GW00363210

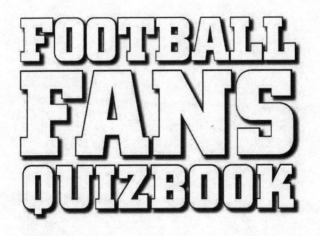

# FOOTBALL FANS QUIZBOOK

# FOOTBALL FANS QUIZBOOK

## DAVE BLAKE

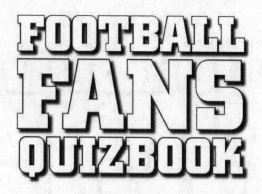

# FOOTBALL FANS QUIZBOOK

All statistics, facts and figures are correct as of 1st August 2008
© Dave Blake

Dave Blake has asserted his rights in accordance with the Copyright, Designs
and Patents Act 1988 to be identified as the author of this work.

Published By:
Pitch Publishing Ltd,
A2 Yeoman Gate,
Durrington BN13 3QZ

Email: info@pitchpublishing.co.uk
Web: www.pitchpublishing.co.uk

First published 2008

All rights reserved. No part of this publication may be reproduced, stored in a
retrieval system, or transmitted in any form or by any means, electronic, mechanical,
photocopying, recording or otherwise, without the prior permission in writing
of the publisher and the copyright owners.

A catalogue record for this book is available from the British Library.

10-digit ISBN: 1-9054113-2-4
13-digit ISBN: 978-1-9054113-2-0
Printed and bound in Great Britain by Cromwell Press

# INTRODUCTION

Is it the Worthington Cup or the Coca Cola Cup – the Milk Cup or the Carling Cup? But hang on a minute – didn't Carling sponsor the Premier League? Or was that Mastercard... or Barclays? And when I say Premier League, do I really mean Premiership? And when I say League Champions, do I mean Premier League or Premiership Champions, or do I mean League Champions as in the Football League – the second tier?

In the last two decades or so, football has gone into re-branding overdrive. But up to the 1990's it was so much simpler. In England it was four divisions numbered 'One', 'Two', 'Three' and 'Four', and whoever won The Championship was, by-and-large, the best team in the country. So for the sake of clarity and continuity, I have attempted in this quiz book to eradicate the "Hang on a minute..." factor.

Therefore, regardless of sponsors, all competitions have been referred to by their generic title (League Cup, Conference etc....). The pre-Premier League divisions (before 1992/93) are always referred to as 'Division 1' through to 'Division 4'. Following the formation of the Premier League, the top division, regardless of the official title, is always referred to as the 'Premier League', and in the face of constant re-branding, the other three divisions have been bracketed with reference to which tier they have become ('Championship' [2nd tier], League 1 [3rd tier] and League 2 [4th tier])

On the international scene, Europe's foremost international tournament began life in 1960 as the UEFA European Nations Cup. In 1968 it became the UEFA European Football Championship. But it wasn't until it came to England that it was simply referred to as Euro '96. This is the truncated title that I have used for each of the tournaments which have taken place.

As far as continental clubs are concerned, I have used their more commonly known English names (Internazionale become Inter Milan, 1.FC Koln become FC Cologne, Sporting Clube de Portugal become Sporting Lisbon etc...).

It now appears to be a fine line between being a 'Manager' and being a 'Coach'. So, in the main, I have put them all in the same basket as 'managers' – though there are odd exceptions where the word 'coach' seems more appropriate. I've no idea why.

Finally, all information included in this quiz book was correct as of August 1st 2008. However, if I have made any glaring errors or omissions, I have little doubt that I will be told, and will humbly bow to those with a greater knowledge.

**Dave Blake**
**August 1st, 2008**

# ME! ME! ME! – I

### From the following description, guess who I am.

With my imperial name, it was only natural that I should join a club with a military moniker, even though I was born in enemy territory. I spent nine years playing a bit part and, because of my stints coming off the bench, got the nickname 'The Five Minute Man'. I gained caps at under-21 level, but was prone to high-profile errors that probably cost my club a Wembley trophy against some hat makers. I then became a bit of a journeyman with 'Rs', Robins, Diamonds, Jags and two U's, as well as a chapter in a high-temperature confessional football book.

## SOME QUESTIONS ABOUT... EVERTON

1. Old Ma Bushell invented the Everton toffees and sold them at Goodison Park. But what did her rival, Old Mother Noblett invent?

2. Which 'double' did they win under Howard Kendall in 1984/85?

3. Which country used Everton's state-of-the-art training ground at Bellefield as their base during the 1966 World Cup tournament?

## THE 2000s – I

1. In 2001 what did Birmingham, Arsenal and Alavés have in common?

2. In October 2001 former referee Ken Aston died at the age of 86. What major innovation did he introduce to world football in 1970, and what was this innovation based on?

3. Who officially opened MK Dons new stadium in November 2007 – was it Tony Blair, the Queen or The Spice Girls?

## PRAWN SANDWICH ANYONE? – I

**If you were sharing an executive box with these celebrity fans, which two teams might you be watching?**

1. Singer/songwriter Chris de Burgh and surreal comedian Vic Reeves.

2. Tony 'Baldrick' Robinson and bluesy pop singer Alison Moyet.

3. Campaigning former MP Tony Benn and Mike "this is me" Yarwood.

## SOME QUESTIONS ABOUT... ROTHERHAM UNITED

1. What denied Rotherham a place in the top flight in 1954/55?

2. Who did they meet in the first ever League Cup Final in 1960/61?

3. Which Bermudan international scored 70 goals in 209 appearances for the club in two spells between 1989 and 1996?

## WORLD CUP – I

1. Mexico 1970 saw the introduction of red and yellow cards. How many red cards were shown during the 32 games that took place – was it two, eight or none at all?

2. What musical tradition was started prior to Italia '90?

3. The Olympiastadion in Munich, built for the 1972 Olympic Games, remained unused during the 2006 World Cup. But which two major international football finals had the stadium hosted in previous years?

## HE SAID WHAT? – I

### Who are responsible for these quotes?

1. "Football is simple, but the most difficult thing is to play simple football."

2. "I wouldn't say I was the best manager in the business. But I was in the top one."

3. "Mind you, I've been here during the bad times too. One year we came second."

## SOME QUESTIONS ABOUT...
## QUEENS PARK RANGERS

1. Which two motor racing magnates bought the club in 2007/08?

2. What 'double' did they win in 1966/67?

3. Between Tommy Docherty in 1980 and Luigi De Canio in 2007, the club appointed 14 different managers. Of those, eight also played for the club at some stage during their career. Name them.

## STUART PEARCE

1. In 1985 Nott'm Forest acquired Pearce and another player from Coventry. Who was the central defender in the £300,000 deal in which Pearce was perceived as the makeweight – was it Ian Butterworth, Franz Carr or Hans Segers?

2. As Man C manager in 2006, what lucky mascot did Pearce keep by the home dugout during a mildly successful run of results?

3. Early in his career at Forest, what did Pearce advertise in the match-day programme?

## STAT-TASTIC! – I

### Identify the player from the following career statistics.

Born: Macclesfield.
League Career Span: 1998/99 to the present.
International Caps: 26 apps – 14 goals (to date).

| CLUB/NICKNAME | LEAGUE APPS | GOALS |
|---|---|---|
| Spurs | 0 | 0 |
| The Hamlet {loan} | 6 | 1 |
| IFK Hässleholm (loan} | 8 | 3 |
| R's | 42 | 10 |
| Pompey | 37 | 18 |
| Villans | 37 | 6 |
| Canaries {loan} | 15 | 4 |
| Saints | 27 | 12 |
| Pool | 85 | 22 |
| Pompey (to date) | 0 | 0 |

## SOME QUESTIONS ABOUT... AC MILAN

1. Which club do they share the San Siro Stadium with?

2. Two English expatriates from Nottingham founded Associazione Calcio Milan in 1899. But as well as football, what other sport did they initially play?

3. In the 1980s they embarked on their greatest period of success following the signing of three Dutchmen. Name them and the coach that signed them.

## THE 1990s – I

1. Who made a scoring debut at Selhurst Park in May 1997 and struck a legendary goal on the world stage a little over a year later?

2. In 1990/91 which club did Neil Warnock guide to a second successive play-off triumph as they climbed from Division 3 to Division 1 – was it Swindon, Notts Co or Barnsley?

3. In November 1994 Spurs, Everton and Aston Villa all sacked their managers within nine days of each other. Name the managers.

## STRIKING FOR GLORY – I

### For which clubs and in which season did these deadly duos make defenders lives a misery?

1. Alan Warboys [22 goals] & Bruce Bannister [18 goals].

2. Jamie Cureton [23 goals] & Chris Iwelumo [18 goals].

3. Mark Bright [25 goals] & Ian Wright [20 goals].


## SOME QUESTIONS ABOUT... STOKE CITY

1. In which season did Stoke last compete in the top division prior to their promotion in 2007/08 – was it 1976/77, 1984/85 or 1998/99?

2. In 1925 the town of Stoke was granted 'city status' by George V. The football club changed their name accordingly. But what were Stoke City known as before this?

3. Three of England's 1966 World Cup winning squad spent time with Stoke during their career. Who were they?


## THE FA CUP – I

1. As of 2007/08, two clubs have contested 25 FA Cup semi-finals each. Who are they?

2. In 1970/71 Oxford lost 3-1 to Leicester in a 5th Round replay. But which future manager and pundit scored Oxford's consolation goal?

3. Who were the last club to win the FA Cup for the first time?

# WHO'S MISSING? – I

**Below are eight of the starting line-up when Man Utd
beat Benfica 4-1 to win the European Cup in 1967/68.
Name the three missing players.**

___?___ , Shay Brennan, Tony Dunne, Pat Crerand, Bill Foulkes,
___?___, George Best,  Brian Kidd, Bobby Charlton, ___?___, John
Aston.

## SOME QUESTIONS ABOUT... WIGAN ATHLETIC

1. Having consistently failed to gain admission to the Football League in
the days before automatic promotion and relegation, which league did
Wigan apply to join as an alternative in 1972/73?

2. Which Lancashire club did they eventually replace when voted into
the Football League in 1978/79?

3. When David Whelan bought Wigan, he was widely ridiculed for stating
his ambition to take the club from Division 3 [fourth tier], all the way to
the Premier League. But how many seasons did it actually take – was it
8, 10 or 14?

## STANLEY MATTHEWS

1. Which club did he manage briefly in the late 1960s?

2. How old was he when he rejoined his home town club Stoke in 1961,
and what did he help them to achieve the following season?

3. Where were his ashes buried following his death at the age of 85 in
2000?

## GETTING THERE... – I

**Arriving at the railway station, you jump in a cab. This is the route your taxi takes. But which ground are you heading to?**

It's just under a mile away. Follow Station Rd straight on and into Mill St. Turn right on to New Bedford Rd. Take the first available exit off the roundabout on to Telford Way. Take second available exit off the roundabout on to the A505. Immediately turn left on to Dunstable Rd. Turn left on to Ash Rd and then the first available left on to Maple Rd East. You can jump out there.

## SOME QUESTIONS ABOUT... MIDDLESBROUGH

1. When Gareth Southgate was appointed manager in 2006, which former Sunderland and Oxford boss did he appoint as his assistant?

2. Who made his Football League debut for 'Boro in 1955/56, and went on to score 197 goals in 213 games for the club?

3. Name the three former 'Boro managers (one was a 'caretaker') who have been head coach/assistant-manager for England?

## THE 1980s – I

1. What innovation was introduced to the Football League in 1981/82?

2. Who compiled a report regarding improvements at football grounds following the Hillsborough disaster in 1989?

3. After three promotions in four seasons, which manager led Swansea into the top flight in 1980/81?

## THE BIG JOB – I

### Who had the full-time managers job either side of the following appointments?

1. Arsenal: ___?___ (1984-86) George Graham (1986-95) ___?___(1995-96).

2. Leeds: ___?___ (1980-82) Eddie Gray (1982-85) ___?___(1985-88).

3. Preston: ___?___ (1973-75) Harry Catterick (1975-77) ___?___ (1977-81).

## SOME QUESTIONS ABOUT... BURY

1. Which one of the following players did not begin their league career with Bury. Terry McDermott, Colin Bell, Neville Southall, Lee Dixon, David Nugent or Colin Kazim-Richards?

2. Since 2005/06, which non-league club has used Gigg Lane for their home games?

3. On the opening day of 1994/95, which 38 year-old former England international – at the time between management posts – played one game for Bury in what turned out to be his final outing before hanging up his boots?

## HOME OF THE BRAVE – I

1. Celtic and Rangers are known as the 'Old Firm'. But in the 1980s which two clubs became known as the 'New Firm'?

2. Which former Brighton FA Cup Final scorer was appointed Chief Executive of the Scottish Football Association in June 2007?

3. In the season that Celtic became the first British club to win the European Cup, another club left the Scottish League and died. Who were they?

## SEQUENCES – I

### Who is next in the following sequences?

1. Colin Todd (1990-91), Lennie Lawrence (1991-94), Bryan Robson (1994-2001), ___?___ (2001-06).

2. Chelsea (2003/04), Arsenal (2004/05), Man Utd (2005/06), Chelsea (2006/07), ___?___ (2007/08).

3. Tony Book (Man C – 1968/69), Ron Harris (Chelsea – 1969/70), Frank McLintock (Arsenal – 1970/71), ___?___ (? – 1971/72).

## SOME QUESTIONS ABOUT... CELTIC

1. In 1966/67 Celtic won every major competition they entered. Name them.

2. In 1949 Jamaican-born Gilbert Heron became Celtic's first black player. Although he scored on his debut he would only play three games before moving on. Name his poet/musician/activist son.

3. When Jock Stein took over as manager in 1965 and almost immediately won the Scottish Cup, how many years had Celtic endured without winning a major trophy – was it 3, 7 or 12?

## EUROPEAN SILVERWARE – I

1. Real Madrid beat State de Reims to win the first ever European Cup in 1956. Where was that final played?

2. Name the two Scottish winners of the European Cup-Winners' Cup?

3. What was the UEFA Cup known as before 1972?

## BY MUTUAL CONSENT? – I

### Identify the well-known manager from the following clues.

This steely winger started his career with a sharp edge before joining hooting neighbours. He later transformed into a seabird. But it was with amber pilgrims that he became bossy having initially been signed as a player by a bald eagle. After non-league success he became 'number 2' with the oldest magpies before taking over the hot seat. His coaching abilities were already to the fore and he moved in with owls who he took to the top flight. Struggling white peacocks hired his talents, and within four years he had taken them to the domestic peak. He was eventually appointed to technically mould the future of the national game and had two brief spells picking the three lions. Although still heavily involved in the game his final management role to date was an unhappy period with dark felines.

## SOME QUESTIONS ABOUT... BIRMINGHAM CITY

1. In which year did Birmingham add 'City' to their name – was it 1902, 1916 or 1943?

2. Which major European cup final did they reach in both 1960 and 1961?

3. In 1979 who left Birmingham, and in doing so became the first £1m player to be transferred between English clubs?

## THE 1970s – I

1. In 1972 which club was voted out of the Football League, and which Cup 'Giant Killers' replaced them?

2. In April 1979 which future prolific striker made his debut in midfield for 'The Seals' in a Division 3 game against Sheff Wed?

3. Which club did future England manager Graham Taylor guide to the Division 4 title in 1975/76?

## HOW MUCH? – I

1. In 2001 Zinedine Zidane was transferred from Juventus to Real Madrid. What was the alleged transfer fee – was it £28.5m, £46m or £68m?

2. In 1995 a footballer won a European Court of Justice decision concerning freedom of movement for players at the end of their contracts. What was his name and nationality?

3. Who in 1905 became the first player to be transferred for £1,000, and which two north-east clubs were involved in the deal?

## SOME QUESTIONS ABOUT... BLACKPOOL

1. Who would be Blackpool's opponents if they were playing in the M55 derby?

2. How many FA Cup finals did Blackpool compete in between 1948 and 1953 – was it one, three or four?

3. In 1994 which former Bolton and Preston defender took up his first full-time management role in England with Blackpool?

## THE WORLD GAME – I

1. The winners of which two cups usually contested the World Club Championship between 1960 and 2004?

2. Which German club, nicknamed The Billy Goats, won the inaugural Bundesliga in 1963/64 – was it Borussia Monchengladbach, Bayern Munich or FC Cologne?

3. Which five Italian clubs were found guilty of match fixing in 2006?

## ANOTHER BITE AT THE CHERRY? – I

Which six members of the Liverpool team that won the 2005 Champions League Final against AC Milan, also figured in the team that lost to the same opponents, in the same final two years later in 2007?

## SOME QUESTIONS ABOUT... READING

1. Reading were once known as 'The Biscuitmen'. But which biscuit-manufacturing company was a major employer in the town before closing in the 1970s – was it Peak Frean, Huntley & Palmer or McVities?

2. From the start of the 1985/86, how many league games did Reading play before dropping any points?

3. The 1998 biography 'The Greatest Footballer You Never Saw', by Paolo Hewitt and Paul McGuigan, was about which iconic former Reading player?

## JACK'S REPUBLIC

1. In Jack Charlton's two World Cup tournaments as Republic of Ireland manager (1990 and 1994), two players appeared for every minute in all nine games that they played. Who were they?

2. In their opening match of USA '94, the Republic caused what proved to be one of the shocks of the tournament. Who did they beat, and who was the sole scorer?

3. Having qualified from the group stages at Italia '90, the Republic came up against Rumania in the 'Round Of 16'. The Republic won 5-4 on penalties. But who scored the decisive fifth penalty for them?

## SIGN ON THE DOTTED LINE, SON – I

**Name the clubs that the following players
first signed with as professionals.**

1. Chris Sutton.

2. Robbie Savage.

3. Lawrie Sanchez.

## SOME QUESTIONS ABOUT...
## QUEENS PARK, GLASGOW

1. In the first-ever official football international against England in 1872, how many Queens Park players represented Scotland?

2. How many times did they reach the final of the English FA Cup – was it once, twice or four times?

3. Kamel Mansour played in goal for Queens Park between 1937 and 1939, becoming one of the first non-British or Irish players to play in the Scottish leagues. Which North African country did he represent at the 1934 World Cup?

## THE 1960s – I

1. In which season did Spurs become the first 20th century winners of the League and FA Cup 'Double'?

2. Following England's victory in the 1966 World Cup, Bobby Moore, Martin Peters and Geoff Hurst returned to West Ham for the new season. But where in Division 1 did The Hammers finish that season – was it 5th, 16th or 20th?

3. In 1964/65 Leeds were runners-up in two competitions. What were they?

# BIRTH OF A CLUB

**Guess the club from the brief description of their formation.**

Following the success of local club Excelsior, a group of businessmen met at the Napier Arms intent on forming a more competitive football club. New Brompton came into existence as a result, and land was purchased near to a level-crossing. Local dockyard workers helped to build the ground and the first competitive game took place there in 1893. The club, who were re-named in 1913, still play at this location today.

# SOME QUESTIONS ABOUT... SPAIN

1. In 1929 they became the first non-British side to beat England. Where was the game played and what was the score?

2. Between 1964 and 1974, whilst playing for Atlético Madrid, which controversial future national team manager became known as 'Zapatones'?

3. Having taken up Spanish nationality, Ferenc Puskás gained three of his four caps during the 1962 World Cup tournament. But for which other country did he score an astonishing 84 goals in 85 international appearances?

# THREE LIONS – I

1. In the 100 years between 1884 and 1984, how many Home International Championships did England win outright – was it 34, 51 or 68?

2. England were knocked out of the 1970 World Cup in the quarter-finals by W. Germany. It would be twelve years before their next game in the finals. But who were their first opponents in the 1982 tournament?

3. With which Football League clubs did the following England managers play their final league game? Bobby Robson, Steve McClaren, Don Revie, Graham Taylor and Terry Venables.

# LATIN HOMEWORK – I

Three traditional nicknames and mottos. Name the club and translate the motto.

1. Toffees – Nil Satis Nisi Optimum.

2. Potters – Vis Unita Portior.

3. Robins – Salubritas et Eruditio.

# SOME QUESTIONS ABOUT...
## SHAMROCK ROVERS

1. In the preliminary round of the 1957/58 European Cup, which soon to be decimated side did they meet?

2. Where do they currently play their home games – is it Lansdowne Rd, Tolka Park or Croke Park?

3. One of the following players never turned out for the club. Which one; Johnny Giles, John Aldridge, Jim Beglin and Eamon Dunphy?

# DIDIER DROGBA

1. With which French club, more associated with motor sport, did Drogba sign his first professional contract in 1999?

2. What nickname did Drogba have as a child – was it Tonto, Toto or Tito?

3. Drogba's cousin Olivier Tébily played for three British clubs between 1999 and 2008. Name them.

# INTO THE LEAGUE! – I

### Guess the club from the details of their first ever home league game.

OPPOSITION: Northwich Victoria.
LEAGUE: Division 2.
DATE: September 3rd 1892.
HOME GROUND: Abbey Park.
COLOURS: cardinal red and blue halved shirts, white knickers, black stockings.

# SOME QUESTIONS ABOUT...
# MANCHESTER UNITED

1. At the end of 1973.74, Denis Law famously scored for Man C against Man Utd with a cheeky back-heel. This gave City a 1-0 victory and confirmed the relegation of their rivals to Division 2. But would United have gone down anyway had they avoided defeat in this match?

2. Name the seven former 'Ferguson' players managing in the Premier League/Football League at the close of 2007/08.

3. In December 1986, who was the ex-United player who signed goalkeeper Fraser Digby for Swindon, thus making him Alex Ferguson's first transfer transaction as United manager?

# PRE-1960s – I

1. A legendary Man Utd, Aston Villa and Republic of Ireland defender was born on December 4th 1959. Who was it?

2. Which now-defunct South Wales club finished bottom of Division 3 (South) in 1924/25 – was it Merthyr Town, Cardiff Wanderers or Newport Pagnell?

3. West London clubs occupied the bottom position of both Division 1 and Division 2 in 1951/52. Who were they?

## 1966 AND ALL THAT – I

1. In August 1960 FIFA met in Rome to decide on the hosts for the 1966 tournament. England gained 34 votes. Which other European country's bid came in second with 27 votes?

2. England defeated Portugal in the semi-final at Wembley after the FA managed to get the game moved from another stadium. Which one?

3. What was the name of the dog that found the Jules Rimet trophy after it had been stolen from a stamp exhibition in London – was it Pickles, Fido or Steve?

## SOME QUESTIONS ABOUT... ALDERSHOT TOWN

1. In 1985 which former England striker made five league appearances for the club whilst on loan from Millwall?

2. How many seasons passed between Aldershot resigning from the Football League and Aldershot Town returning – was it 9, 15 or 21?

3. Which QPR FA Cup finalist (1981/82) managed the Shots into the Football League in 2007/08?

## EURO CHAMPIONSHIPS – I

1. Two members of the England Euro '80 squad were playing for clubs based in W. Germany. Name them both and the clubs they played for?

2. What was unique about Otto Rehhagel when he managed Greece to victory in the 2004 tournament?

3. Who hosted the very first Euro championship finals in 1960, and how many teams competed?

## ODD ONE OUT – I

### From this list, name the one club that Steve Claridge has not played for.

Bournemouth, Crystal Palace, Aldershot, Cambridge, Luton, Birmingham, Leicester, Portsmouth, Wolves, Millwall, Brighton, Brentford, Wycombe, Gillingham, Bradford C or Walsall.

## SOME QUESTIONS ABOUT... WYCOMBE WANDERERS

1. Which trade were the founders of Wycombe employed in?

2. In which two seasons did they reach the semi-finals of the FA Cup and the League Cup?

3. Which future Premier League manager took them into the Football League in 1992/93?

## TODAY'S THE DAY – I

### Identify the major news story that occurred on the day when the following events were happening in the world of football.

In the Champions League Michael Owen's goal secures a draw for Liverpool against Boevista, whilst Arsenal lose to Real Mallorca, where Ashley Cole is sent-off. In the League Cup, Division 2 (3rd tier) Reading defeat Premier League West Ham on penalties. Future Celtic scoring-machine Scott McDonald makes his senior debut in the UK as Southampton defeat Brighton. And on the same day that Middlesbrough are refused a work-permit for Celta Vigo striker Benni McCarthy, a Riverside all-time-low crowd of 3,915 witness Steve McClaren's team beat Northampton.
Meanwhile in Manhattan and Arlington...

## ME! ME! ME! – II

### From the following description, guess who I am.

In my career that spanned over 30 years, I never played for any of the so-called 'glamour' clubs, but I did appear in three World Cup tournaments and two European Cup wins. Starting as a fox-cub, I studied under the safest mentor in the business. He took up pottery and I was destined to do the same. I then became a 'young man' in a woody area where plaudits came in abundance. I moved in with some resurgent saints and then penned myself in with male sheep. In my fourth decade and with a record number of caps I managed pilgrims, but still hankered to play. Although I made one appearance with some trotters I had non-playing sessions with now-defunct madmen, midland sky-blues and cockney tools. I finally made my landmark 1,000th appearance playing for exotic eastern capitalists.

## SOME QUESTIONS ABOUT... HULL CITY

1. In 1972, Spain were the visitors for the first and only full international played at Boothferry Park. But who were the 'home' team?

2. Who would Hull be playing in the 'Humber Derby'?

3. In 1909/10 what colours did they wear as first choice kit – was it all pink, all black or Union Jack design shirts?

## THE 2000s – II

1. In 2006/07 what was unique about Oxford Utd's appearance in the Conference following their relegation from the Football League?

2. In 2001/02 Sheff Utd hosted WBA in an ill-tempered Division 1 (2nd tier) game. When the game was abandoned after 82 minutes with WBA leading 3-0, how many players did Sheff Utd still have on the pitch?

3. At the beginning of 2005/06, which two clubs opened new stadiums?

## STARTING XI – I

**From this opening-day-of-the-season starting-eleven,
name the club and the season.**

Parkes, Clement, Watson, Venables, Evans, Hazell, Busby, Francis,
O'Rourke, Leach, Givens.

## SOME QUESTIONS ABOUT... HIBERNIAN

1. Hibernia is the Roman name for what?

2. What do children's author Enid Blyton, and the post-war Hibs forward line of Smith, Johnstone, Reilly, Turnbull and Ormond have in common?

3. In their song 'Cap in Hand', The Proclaimers sing;
"I can understand why ___?___ lie so lowly
They could save a lot of points by signing Hibs' goalie."
Who are the missing club?

## WORLD CUP – II

1. In May 2004 South Africa won the right to stage the 2010 World Cup by gaining 14 votes. Morocco came second with ten votes. But which country came third in the ballot, and how many votes did they gain?

2. What nationality was Jules Rimet, founder of the World Cup tournament, and what position did he hold within the game from 1921 to 1954?

3. What did the 1994 World Cup Final have in common with the 1970 final?

## HE SAID WHAT? – II

### Who are responsible for these quotes?

1. "England did nothing in the World Cup, so why are they bringing books out? 'We got beat in the quarter-finals, I played like shit, here's my book'. Who wants to read that? I don't."

2. "When the seagulls follow the trawler, it is because they think sardines will be thrown into the sea."

3. "If a Frenchman goes on about seagulls, trawlers and sardines, he's called a philosopher. I'd just be called a short Scottish bum talking crap."

## SOME QUESTIONS ABOUT... PORTSMOUTH

1. One theory for the clubs nickname derives from 1781 when some Portsmouth sailors climbed Pompey's Pillar and became known as the 'Pompey boys'. Where is Pompey's Pillar – is it in Alexandria, Egypt, Cádiz in Spain or Alexandroupolis in Greece?

2. When Harry Redknapp took over as manager in 2002, who became his assistant?

3. Who was the last Pompey player to represent England at a World Cup finals tournament – was it Darren Anderton, Steve Stone or Jimmy Dickinson?

## ROY KEANE

1. In 1991, which England international did Keane displace in the centre of the Nott'm Forest midfield?

2. In 1992, which Lancashire club was on the brink of signing Keane from Nott'm Forest when Alex Ferguson jumped-in with a better offer?

3. Who did Keane replace as Man Utd club captain in 1997?

## "YOU'LL NEVER TAKE THE HOME END!" – I

**A well-known 'Home End' – past or present.
Name the club it belongs to.**

1. Hammersmith End.

2. Trent End.

3. North Bank.


## SOME QUESTIONS ABOUT...
## AJAX OF AMSTERDAM

1. What did Ajax earn the right to do after winning the European Cup in 1973?

2. The great line-up of the early '70s – Stuy, Suurbier, Hulshoff, Blankenburg, Krol, Haan, Neeskens, Mühren, Swart, Cruyff, Keizer and Suurendonk – was sometimes known by what biblical name?

3. Who was the last Englishman to manage Ajax – was it Bobby Robson, Vic Buckingham or Roy Hodgson?


## THE 1990s – II

1. How many managers did Swansea have during the 1995/96 season – was it five, seven or none at all?

2. On September 3rd 1999 Newcastle appointed Bobby Robson to succeed Ruud Gullit as manager. Fifteen days later they swamped a Yorkshire club 8-0. Who were these opponents and who scored five of the goals?

3. In 1991/92, which two Yorkshire clubs finished first and third in the last-ever Football League Championship before the creation of the Premier League?

## STRIKING FOR GLORY – II

1. What international goalscoring achievement do Thierry Henry, Jurgen Klinsmann, Vladimir Smicer and Nuno Gomes share?

2. In 1966/67, Ron Davies, Bobby Gould, Rodney Marsh and Ernie Phythain were the top scorers in the four English divisions. Which clubs were they playing for?

3. Who is the only English player to score in three separate World Cup tournaments?

## SOME QUESTIONS ABOUT... BARNSLEY

1. Barnsley have reached the FA Cup Final twice (1909/10 and 1911/12). Although both games went to replays, the initial final games were played at which ground?

2. In 1953 which future England striker joined Man Utd from Barnsley, only to become a victim in the 1958 Munich air crash?

3. Gerry Taggart is their most capped international. For which country?

## FA CUP – II

1. Who were the two losing semi-finalists in the 2007/08 FA Cup?

2. Which Leeds born Scottish international came off the bench in the 1988/89 final to score twice for Everton against Liverpool?

3. What distinction does 19th century Old Harrovian Morton Peto Betts have?

## CUP FINAL COLOURS – I

### What colours did these clubs wear
### in the following FA Cup Finals?

1. WBA (v Everton) in 1967/68.

2. Crystal Palace (v Man Utd) in the 1989/90 replay.

3. Liverpool (v Man Utd) in 1995/96.

## SOME QUESTIONS ABOUT... CARDIFF CITY

1. Cardiff were born out of another sports club in 1899. Which sport did that club play?

2. In 1959, 62,634 people crammed in to Ninian Park for an international. Which two countries were playing?

3. In November 1965, which future international striker became their youngest ever player at 16 years and 236 days?

## ALLY'S TARTAN ARMY

1. Which stadium did the squad parade around in an open-top bus prior to their flight out to Argentina for the 1978 World Cup tournament?

2. What was manager Ally McLeod's response after a journalist had asked him what he planned to do after Scotland had won the 1978 World Cup?

3. Which WBA winger was sent home following Scotland's opening game defeat to Peru, after it was revealed he had taken a banned stimulant to fend off a cold?

## GETTING THERE – II

**Arriving at the railway station, you jump in a cab. This is the route your taxi takes. But which ground are you heading to?**

It's just about a mile away. Turn left on to Railway Drive and into Fryer St. Take the third available right on to Broad St and then follow the St Patricks Ring Rd. Take the first available right on to the A4150 and follow the St Andrews Ring Rd and then turn right onto Waterloo Rd. The stadium is just on your right.

## SOME QUESTIONS ABOUT... OXFORD UNITED

1. Before becoming Oxford Utd in 1960, what were the club known as?

2. In 1983, controversial business tycoon Robert Maxwell proposed a merger with Reading. What would the new club have been called and who was lined up as manager?

3. Which 2008 'Humberside hero' did they sign from Aberdeen in 1998?

## THE 1980s – II

1. Which two far-reaching and tragic disasters dominated the 1984/85 season?

2. At the end of 1988/89, when Arsenal won the Football League title with almost the very last kick of the domestic season, which players scored the two goals that beat Liverpool in a classic showdown at Anfield?

3. Which two founding-members of the Football League were relegated to Division 3 at the end of the 1982/83 season?

## NET MINDERS – I

### On the opening day of the 1978/79 season these were the 22 goalkeepers on duty in Division 1. Name the clubs they represented.

Kevin Keelan, Tony Godden, Paddy Roche, Peter Bonetti, Barry Daines, Phil Parkes, Jimmy Rimmer, Paul Cooper, Peter Shilton, Paul Bradshaw, Joe Corrigan, John Shaw, Les Sealey, Pat Jennings, Jim Stewart, Jim Montgomery, Peter Wells, John Middleton, Ray Clemence, Jim McDonagh, George Wood, David Harvey.

## SOME QUESTIONS ABOUT... BLACKBURN ROVERS

1. Blackburn are one of only three clubs to be founder members of both the Football League and the Premier League. Name the other two.

2. Which future football club owner broke his leg in the first half of the 1959/60 FA Cup Final defeat against Wolves?

3. In 1996/97, which Sampdoria manager u-turned on a promise to become Rovers new manager – joining Lazio instead?

## HOME OF THE BRAVE – II

1. In 1949/50 Rangers played Hibs in a title-decider at Ibrox. What was the crowd – was it 101,000, 134,000 or was it played behind closed door?

2. In 1928 Scotland beat England 5-1 at Wembley. The reporter for the Athletic News wrote 'England were not merely beaten. They were bewildered – run to a standstill, made to appear utterly inferior by a team whose play was as cultured and beautiful as I ever expect to see'. What did that mythical Scottish team become known as?

3. Which two Spanish clubs contested the 2007 UEFA Cup Final at Hampden Park?

# SEQUENCES – II

### Who is next in the following sequences?

1. Plymouth, Plymouth, Plymouth, ___?___.

2. Mariano García Remón, Vanderlei Luxemburgo, Juan Ramón López Caro, ___?___.

3. Aston Villa, Norwich, Birmingham, ___?___.

# SOME QUESTIONS ABOUT...
# DAGENHAM & REDBRIDGE

1. Formed in 1992, their origins can be traced back to four former FA Trophy/FA Amateur Cup winners. Name them.

2. Aside from the Daggers, only two other clubs from Essex have played at Football League level. Name them.

3. In another previous incarnation, what championship did Redbridge Forest win in 1990/91 – was it the Vauxhall Conference, the Metropolitan League or the Isthmian League?

# EUROPEAN SILVERWARE – II

1. In the Champions League Final of 2007/08, five of the players who participated spent some time at West Ham earlier in their career. Name them.

2. To date, only one player has appeared in more than 150 games in the three major competitions. Name him.

3. Wembley Stadium has hosted five European Cup or Champions League Finals. There have been two English, one Italian, one Dutch and one Spanish winner. Name them.

# BY MUTUAL CONSENT? – II

### Identify the well-known manager from the following clues.

This hard working central defender began with local hoops, winning a championship before moving south to an academic abbey. Spells with west country robins and small rodents in old-fashioned happy greenery followed before returning north of the border to an athletic club with an even-golfing moniker. Academia briefly beckoned again but this time closer to his roots. He combined coaching and playing for lilywhites before assuming a blue hot seat. Having turned down the opportunity to play second fiddle to a red knight, he took up the challenge to revive these tired purveyors of chewy confectionary.

## SOME QUESTIONS ABOUT... WORKINGTON

1. Who did they replace as a Football League club in 1951 – was it Wigan Borough, New Brighton or Nelson?

2. Which legendary manager was in charge between January 1954 and December 1955?

3. Which England international goalkeeper began his career with the Reds?

## THE 1970s – II

1. Which three founder members of the Football League occupied the top three positions of Division 3 at the end of season 1972/73?

2. Having already made six appearances for QPR as a substitute, which striker made his first league start in April 1979, at home to Coventry, and scored a hat-trick?

3. Who was manager Bertie Mee's first team coach when Arsenal won the double in 1970/71?

## WHAT'S IN A NICKNAME? – I

**Guess the club from this description of their nickname.**

A common hard metal that is used to make steel. It is magnetic and is found in very small quantities in food and blood. Its chemical symbol is 'Fe'...

# SOME QUESTIONS ABOUT... BRISTOL ROVERS

1. Between 1986 and 1996, which ground did they play at?

2. Formed in 1883, they were briefly called The Black Arabs. Was it because they wore black and played next door to the Arab Rugby Club, was it because the players were predominantly Arabian sailors, or was it because they were formed by a mediocre music hall double act called 'The Black Arabs'?

3. Which former England captain had two spells as manager?

# THE WORLD GAME – II

1. Which two former French national coaches have managed clubs in the Premier League?

2. Which new Ajax manager further refined the art of 'Total Football' following the departure of Rinus Michels to Barcelona in 1971 – was it Ernst Happel, Stefan Kovács or Leo Beenhakker?

3. The Austrian national stadium is named after a man who, amongst other honours, played 51 times for his country, coached Holland to a runners-up place in the World Cup and took both Feyenoord and Hamburg to European Cup glory – was it Leo Beenhakker, Stefan Kovács or Ernst Happel?

## HOW MUCH? – II

1. Name the two players – one a 'makeweight' – and the clubs involved in the first £200,000 English transfer in March 1970?

2. In 1971 which WBA and Scotland midfielder was on the verge of signing for Don Revie's Leeds for £170,000, when it was discovered that he had a suspected hole-in-the-heart condition – was it Len Cantello, Asa Hartford or Bobby Hope?

3. In 1995 Dennis Bergkamp became a Gunner, costing £7.5m. But which club was he signed from?

## SOME QUESTIONS ABOUT...
## MANCHESTER CITY

1. Who was signed from Bury in 1966 and became known as 'King of the Kippax'?

2. In a 1987/88 Division 2 fixture, City's Paul Stewart, Tony Adcock and David White had the rare distinction of all scoring hat-tricks. Who were they playing and what was the final score – was it Huddersfield (10-1), Shrewsbury (12-2) or Oldham (9-2)?

3. Which other two clubs did Thaksin Shinawatra allegedly try to buy before his purchase of City in 2007?

## KENNY DALGLISH

1. Which team did he grow up supporting?

2. In 1974/75 Dalglish was made captain of Celtic. What trophies did he lead them to in that season?

3. He scored 30 goals at international level, but who does he share this record with?

## SIGN ON THE DOTTED LINE, SON... – II

**Name the clubs that the following players
first signed with as professionals.**

1. John Hartson
2. Jeff Astle
3. Thierry Henry

## SOME QUESTIONS ABOUT... ACCRINGTON

1. They are often mistakenly associated with Football League founders Accrington FC or the Accrington Stanley who resigned from the Football League in 1962. But when was the current Accrington Stanley formed – was it 1963, 1968 or 1999?

2. In the inaugural Football League season of 1888/89 there were 12 clubs competing. Aside from Accrington FC, how many of the other clubs no longer exist?

3. In an unlikely coincidence, the team that replaced Accrington Stanley in the Football League in 1962 were the same team that they themselves replaced when promoted from the Conference in 2006. Name them.

## THE 1960s – II

1. Which Stamford Bridge legend was born in Sardinia in July 1966, exactly two weeks before Italy were humiliated by North Korea in the World Cup?

2. In 1961, what did Man Utd scout Bob Bishop write when he telegrammed Matt Busby from Belfast to inform him about the 15 year-old George Best?
a) "He's nothing to write home about."
b) "He's OK. Maybe one for the future."
c) "I think I've found you a genius."

3. In 1960/61 Spurs became only the third club to win the League and FA Cup. But what happened that same season to Preston – the first club to achieve the coveted 'double'?

# MR CHAIRMAN – I

### Name these well known chairmen.

1. If you wanted a ticket for anything – including the Queen's Garden Party – this east Londoner could sort it out for you...

2. This English entrepreneur and businessman got into a habit of firing would-be assistants in a very public way...

3. This Tanzanian-born businessman, who gained a reputation as a 'merchant of misery', took over run-down hostels and hotels, while local councils paid him to fill them with homeless people and asylum seekers...

# SOME QUESTIONS ABOUT... GILLINGHAM

1. Which East Anglian club did they lose their Football League status to in 1937/38, and when did they regain that status?

2. Tony Pulis led them to the Division 3 Play-Off Final in 1998/99. With two minutes left they were leading 2-0, only for their opponents to score twice, and go on to win the game in a penalty shoot-out. Who were their opponents?

3. Who became the first and only Gillingham player to appear in a World Cup final tournament?

# THREE LIONS – II

1. In February 1882, England played Ireland in Belfast and recorded their biggest victory to date. What was the score?

2. Which two former England managers were born in Dagenham, Essex?

3. Peter Shilton gained 125 caps for England. But who is the next most-capped keeper for England?

## STAT-TASTIC – II

**Identify the player from the following career statistics.**

Born: Oxford.
League Career Span: 1983/84 to 2004/05.
International Caps: 43 apps – 2 goals.

| CLUB/NICKNAME | LEAGUE APPS | GOALS |
|---|---|---|
| Gunners | 22 | 0 |
| Seagulls (Loan) | 23 | 1 |
| Villans | 112 | 3 |
| Toffee's | 96 | 0 |
| Gunners | 310 | 4 |
| Foxes | 17 | 0 |
| Royals | 5 | 0 |

# SOME QUESTIONS ABOUT... CARLISLE UNITED

1. Which clubs demise saved Carlisle from relegation to the Conference in 1991/92?

2. Which future legendary manager made his Football League debut for Carlisle against Rochdale on New Years Eve 1932?

3. What did chairman Michael Knighton promise the Brunton Park faithful in 1993?

# JIMMY GREAVES

1. In 1961, which English club made an audacious bid to sign the 21 year-old Greaves just before he went from Chelsea to AC Milan – was it Newcastle, Spurs or Southend?

2. With which future-league team did he finish his career in 1979?

3. Who was 'Saint' to his 'Greavsie' on ITV Saturday lunchtimes between 1985 and 1992?

## STARTING XI – II

**From this opening-day-of-the-season starting-eleven,
name the club and the season.**

Hislop, Watson, Beresford, Batty, Howey, Albert, Lee, Gillespie, Shearer, Ferdinand, Ginola.

## SOME QUESTIONS ABOUT... SUNDERLAND

1. When they won their last Football League title in 1935/36, they became the last club, to date, to do what?

2. Sunderland won the FA Cup in 1972/73. Since then only two other clubs have equalled their achievement of lifting the trophy while playing outside the top tier of English football. Name them.

3. In 2006, Mick McCarthy was sacked in March and Roy Keane was appointed in August. There were two caretaker managers between them. Who were they?

## PRE-1960s – II

1. In season 1900/01, which two clubs from the same east-midlands city finished third and fourth in Division 1?

2. In 1921 the English Football Association banned women from playing the game on Association members' pitches. What reasons did they give?
a) It was not cost effective to play these games.
b) The game, as played by women, was distasteful.
c) Association members' pitches would be ruined by over-use.

3. In season 1956/57, name the two East Anglian rivals who finished at opposite ends of which division?

## EURO '96 AND ALL THAT... – I

1. In December 1995, which two countries played-off at Anfield to determine the 16th team to compete in the tournament?

2. What would the consequences have been had Patrick Kluivert not scored a consolation goal for Holland in England's remarkable 4-1 victory in the final Group A game?

3. What did Turkey, Italy and Spain have in common?

## SOME QUESTIONS ABOUT...
## RUSHDEN & DIAMONDS

1. Which millionaire amalgamated Irthlingborough Diamonds and Rushden Town in 1992, and what famous footware company did he own?

2. Which FA Cup winner with Ipswich and Arsenal led them into the Football League in 2000/01?

3. What did the groundstaff introduce in each corner of Nene Park to deter birds from nesting in the roof – was it scarecrows, model owls or automated klaxons?

## EURO CHAMPIONSHIPS II

1. Which two teams contested the opening game of the 2004 tournament in Portugal – and would come face-to-face again later on?

2. Which European minnows, having disposed of Holland, finally got knocked out of Euro '64 in a quarter-final replay against Denmark?

3. When France triumphed in 1984, their midfield of Luis Fernandez, Michel Platini, Alain Giresse and Jean Tigana were known as what?
a) carré magique (magic square).
b) club de culture (culture club).
c) moteur parfait (perfect engine).

## OLD GROUNDS FOR NEW – I

**Which clubs used to play their home games
at the following grounds?**

1. Eastville.

2. Old Showground.

3. Fellows Park.

## SOME QUESTIONS ABOUT...
## HEREFORD UNITED

1. Which giant of Welsh football became their player/manager in the late 60s?

2. Having famously disposed of Newcastle in the FA Cup 3rd Round in 1971/72, which Division 1 club did they come up against in the 4th Round?

3. To date, how many seasons have Hereford spent in English footballs second tier?

## TODAY'S THE DAY – II

**Identify the major news story that occurred on the day when
the following events were happening in the world of football**

Derby, who recently parted company with Dave Mackay, are linked with Shrewsbury boss and former skipper Alan Durban. In the evening fixtures Tranmere beat Reading 2-1 in a match where Steve Death saves a Ronnie Moore penalty, and Stockport prevent Bournemouth from going top of Division 4 with a 1-0 win. Liverpool go into the weekend with a three point lead over Newcastle and Ipswich, and in Division 4 Newport's home game against Halifax goes ahead despite growing financial strife. "The situation looks very dodgy, indeed", says manager Jimmy Scoular. Meanwhile in 'Middle England' – and record stores across Britain...

## ANOTHER BITE AT THE CHERRY? – II

Which five England players appeared in the 1966 World Cup Final against W. Germany, and also played against the same opponents four years later in the World Cup quarter-final game in Mexico?

## SOME QUESTIONS ABOUT... ABERDEEN

1. Dave Halliday led The Dons to the first of their four Scottish League title in 1954/55. But who managed them to the other three titles?

2. In 1980 Pittodrie became the first all-seated, all-covered ground in Britain. What other innovation was introduced at the same stadium by Dons trainer Donald Coleman in the 1920s – was it corner flags, dugouts or plunge baths?

3. Of the players who won the 1982/83 European Cup-Winners' Cup with Aberdeen, three were managing in the English or Scottish Premier League at the conclusion of the 2007/08 season. Name them.

## THE 2000s – III

1. At the conclusion of the 2002/03 season, which club dropped into Division 2 (3rd tier) eleven years after finishing 3rd in the Football League?

2. In August 2006 Gary Taylor-Fletcher scored for Huddersfield in a 3-0 victory over Rotherham. In doing so he inadvertently touched a scoring milestone in Football League history. What was that milestone?

3. In November 2004 which manager resigned from one club and just two weeks later was appointed as boss of his former clubs fiercest rivals?

## TAKING THE MIC – I

### You've seen or heard him on the telly. Guess who it is.

This son of a Methodist minister was born in Salford and educated at a rugby-playing school in Suffolk. His career began with the Barnet Press and the Sheffield Morning Telegraph where he first reported on football. Hired by the BBC in 1968 as a Radio 2 sports presenter, he took over on 'Match of the Day' in 1971. A memorable commentary a year later when non-league Hereford beat Newcastle in an FA Cup replay, effectively launched him into the national consciousness. With well over a thousand commentaries for the BBC, the final on Euro 2008 was his last 'live' commentary.

## SOME QUESTIONS ABOUT...
## MACCLESFIELD TOWN

1. In 1969/70 they became the first team to win what trophy?

2. Which country used Moss Rose – Macclesfield's home ground – as their training base during Euro '96?

3. Which former Man Utd midfielder took the Silkmen into the Football League in 1996/97?

## WORLD CUP – III

1. In 1986 José Batista of Uruguay was sent off in the Group E game between Uruguay and Scotland. How long into the game was it – 8 seconds, 17 seconds or 56 seconds?

2. Which two countries contested the 2002 Third-Place match?

3. Why did 1930 winners Uruguay decline to compete in the 1934 tournament held in Italy?

## HE SAID WHAT? – III

### Who are responsible for these quotes?

1. "Football is a simple game; twenty-two men chase a ball for ninety minutes and at the end, the Germans always win."

2. "That was a goal good enough to win the league, the cup, the Charity Shield, the World Cup and even the Grand National!"

3. "Even when they had Moore, Hurst and Peters, West Ham's average finish was about seventeenth. It just shows how crap the other eight of us were."

## SOME QUESTIONS ABOUT...
## NORTHAMPTON TOWN

1. Up until 1994 when they moved to Sixfields, who did the Cobblers share their home ground with?

2. Which manager, who took both Huddersfield and Arsenal to two League titles each, started his managerial career with Northampton in 1907 – was it George Allison, Tom Whittaker or Herbert Chapman?

3. How many promotions and relegations did they experience in the 1960s?

## WAYNE ROONEY

1. Which Everton striker was his boyhood hero?

2. Which squad number did he retain throughout his career at Everton – was it '8', '18' or '27'?

3. In the Euro 2004 quarter-final England faced Portugal. Rooney was sent-off for allegedly stamping on a Portuguese opponent, who would move to a Premier League club soon after. Who was it?

## AT THE MOVIES – I

### Three plots from football-based movies. Name them.

1. A team of allied Prisoners of War prepare for a match to be played in Paris against their captors, Nazi Germany. But there are plans afoot for a daring escape...

2. Ninety-one minutes long and filmed in 'real-time'. A documentary focusing on one man during a La Liga game in 2005.

3. A charity match in North London between a top professional side and a touring amateur side is cut short when a player collapses and dies. It is left to Inspector Slade of Scotland Yard to track down the killer...

## SOME QUESTIONS ABOUT...
## BRADFORD PARK AVENUE

1. They were voted out of the Football League in 1970. Who replaced them?

2. Which former England manager began his professional career with them in 1945?

3. When Tom Maley became manager in 1911, they changed their colours to green and white. Why?

## THE 1990s – III

1. In 1992/93, which former England winger was voted 'Player of the Year' by the Football Writers Association having helped his club to reach both the FA Cup and League Cup Finals?

2. When goalkeeper Jimmy Glass scored the dramatic 90th minute equaliser that preserved Carlisle's league status in 1998/99, which club was he on loan from – was it Crystal Palace, Swindon or Man Utd?

3. In July 1990, which Slovakian doctor became the first foreign manager to take charge of a top division club in England?

## STRIKING FOR GLORY – III

1. Which former Leeds and Man Utd striker is the all-time top scorer for Scotland in World Cup final tournaments?

2. With which club does Ally McCoist hold the all-time goalscoring record?

3. Which Argentine striker has the distinction of scoring hat-tricks in two World Cups – 1994 and 1998?

## SOME QUESTIONS ABOUT...
## NEWCASTLE UNITED

1. Between 1905 and 1911, Newcastle played in five FA Cup finals. How many of these did they win?

2. Who are the only two Newcastle players to score over 200 competitive goals for the club?

3. Which former defender scored just one goal in 457 appearances before joining a Football League Championship and European Cup winning club, and eventually replacing their iconic boss?

## FA CUP – III

1. Who were the last Scottish club to appear in the FA Cup?

2. Where was the 1970 final replay between Chelsea and Leeds played?

3. The 2005/06 final saw a 3-3 draw between Liverpool and West Ham which the Merseysider's won 3-1 on penalties. Which veteran scored the Hammers only successful penalty?

## LEAGUE CUP – I

1. The 1963/64 Final was played over two legs at stadiums that no longer exist. Name the two midland clubs involved, and the stadiums?

2. Which Division 4 club reached the 1961/62 Final?

3. Liverpool have won the trophy a record seven times. But when did they win it for the first time – was it 1966/67, 1980/81 or 1994/95?

## SOME QUESTIONS ABOUT...
## SOUTHEND UNITED

1. In January 2006 which player, later sold to Wolves, scored their 5,000th league goal?

2. In 1970, which future England caretaker began his career at Roots Hall?

3. Which manager signed Frank Lampard Snr. from West Ham in 1985?

## BINGHAM'S BOYS

1. In Billy Bingham's two World Cup tournaments as N. Ireland manager (1982 and 1986), a Canadian-born ex-Man Utd defender was the only player to appear for every minute in all eight games that they played. Who was he?

2. Over the two World Cup's, they scored a total of seven goals. Gerry Armstrong scored three and Billy Hamilton two in the 1984 tournaments. In the 1986 tournament Norman Whiteside and Colin Clarke scored one apiece. But which club sides were they all playing for at the time?

3. Which two players, who would both later become club managers, captained N. Ireland to the respective tournaments in 1982 and 1986?

## GETTING THERE – III

**Arriving at the railway station, you jump in a cab. This is the route your taxi takes. But which ground are you heading to?**

It's about a mile away. Follow Railway St and then turn left on to Curzon St. Immediately turn left on to Active Way and take the second available right on to the A682. Take the first available exit off the roundabout on to Yorkshire St and follow straight on to Harry Potts Way. The ground is on your left.

## SOME QUESTIONS ABOUT... WIMBLEDON

1. What unique 'double' did they achieve when they beat Liverpool in the 1987/88 FA Cup Final?

2. When Dean Holdsworth signed from Brentford in 1992, what did chairman Sam Hammam promise him if he scored 20 goals in a season?

3. In 1974/75, the then non-league Wimbledon held reigning League champions Leeds to a draw at Elland Road in the FA Cup 4th Round. However, they lost the replay by a solitary own-goal at Selhurst Park in front of over 40,000 spectators. Which future Dons manager scored that own goal?

## THE 1980s – III

1. In May 1986 which former 'Busby Babe' took over as Carlisle manager?

2. Which 'same-city' clubs were relegated to Division 3 in 1980/81?

3. Between 1982 and 1997, Oldham only had two managers. Both were former Everton strikers. Name them.

## ME! ME! ME! – III

### From the following description, guess who I am.

Although I was always seen as a maverick, nobody could say I was short of flair and ability. Beginning with local citizens, I got shaken for a while and then settled with railway workers. Then it was up to the extreme north-west before successfully replacing a legendary number '10' at capital hoops. I played under three different managers for my five international caps and I'm often told it should have been more but – to tell you the truth – I was a bit too fond of the birds and the nags. Briefly played under 'Old Big 'Ed' before winding down with far-eastern capitalists and pollen-collectors.

## SOME QUESTIONS ABOUT... SCARBOROUGH

1. Which future Premier League club did Scarborough beat in the 1972/73 FA Trophy Final?

2. Who managed them into the Football League in 1986/87 – was it Sam Allardyce, Neil Warnock or Jimmy Sirrel?

3. In 1988, the Seamer Rd Athletic Ground became the McCain Stadium. What was its culinary nickname?

## HOME OF THE BRAVE – III

1. In 2007/08 Walter Smith (Rangers) became the Scottish Football Writers' 'Manager of the Year' for a record sixth time. When did he first win it and which club was he managing?

2. Which two future Scottish managers played in the Falkirk forward line in the early 1970s?

3. When Rangers won the title in 1974/75, it broke Celtic's grip on the championship. How many consecutive titles had Celtic won up to then?

## SEQUENCES – III

### Who is next in the following sequences?

1. Man Utd, West Ham, Man Utd, ___?___.

2. Barnet, Accrington Stanley, Dagenham & Redbridge, ___?___.

3. Tommy Docherty, Dave Sexton, Ron Atkinson, ___?___.

# SOME QUESTIONS ABOUT...
# TOTTENHAM HOTSPUR

1. Between 1958 and 1974 which of the following trophies did manager Bill Nicholson fail to win – FA Cup, League Championship, League Cup, European Cup-Winners' Cup, Inter-Cities Fairs Cup or UEFA Cup?

2. Spurs are supposedly lucky when a season ends in '1'. Name the competitions they won in 1950/51, 1960/61, 1970/71, 1980/81 and 1990/91?

3. In the 1950s who developed the 'push and run' or 'wall-pass' system that brought Spurs the Division 2 and Division 1 titles in successive seasons – was it Arthur Rowe, Walter Winterbottom or Danny Blanchflower?

# EUROPEAN SILVERWARE – III

1. The venue for the 2008 Champions League Final was the Luzhniki Stadium in Moscow. But which revolutionary was the stadium originally named after?

2. Between 1967/68 and 1972/73 English clubs won the Inter-Cities Fairs Cup/UEFA Cup on each occasion bar one. Who were the Belgian club who beat Arsenal in 1970?

3. Which of the following English clubs never won the European Cup-Winners' Cup – Spurs, Man Utd, Liverpool, Arsenal, Chelsea, West Ham, Everton or Man C?

## PRAWN SANDWICH ANYONE? – II

**If you were sharing an executive box with these celebrity fans, which two teams might you be watching?**

1. Matt 'Little Britain' Lucas and old school comedian Jim Davidson.

2. Morning TV host Lorraine Kelly and Carol 'Changing Rooms' Smillie.

3. Alun 'New Tricks' Armstrong and Geri 'Ginger Spice' Halliwell.

## SOME QUESTIONS ABOUT... CAMBRIDGE UNITED

1. Prior to 1951, when they changed their name to Cambridge United, they partly went under the name of their 'home' ground. What name was it?

2. Who led them to two successive FA Cup quarter-finals in 1989/90 and 1990/91?

3. Which French-born former Cameroon, Senegal, Malaysia, DR Congo and Ghana manager briefly took the reigns at Cambridge in 2004 – was it Aimé Jacquet, Alain Perrin or Claude Le Roy?

## THE 1970s – III

1. By Christmas 1973, which goalkeeper was joint-top scorer for Man Utd with two penalty goals?

2. Before Nott'm Forest's triumph in 1977/78, who were the last club to win the Division 2 and Division 1 title in consecutive seasons?

3. Which London club pushed Liverpool all the way to the 1975/76 Football League Championship?

## BY MUTUAL CONSENT? – III

**Identify the well-known manager from the following clues.**

Having spent almost his entire playing career defending with his local Lombardy devils where he would eventually take on the senior role, he was soon on his way to an old lady where he enjoyed two trophy-strewn periods in office – winning absolutely everything on offer. This had been broken up with half-a-decade with his alma mater's city rivals where he picked up a domestic and yet another European gong. Bavaria beckoned twice, again broken-up with a short spell with Italian islanders. Following a purple patch, he took on national responsibility, which led to two disappointing tournaments. A bright Iberian stadium was the next stop followed by red Germans and high-energy Austrian bulls. He is now charged with re-invigorating European greens.

## SOME QUESTIONS ABOUT... PLYMOUTH ARGYLE

1. What were their nearest and furthest away trips in 2007/08?

2. Which goalkeeper managed them between 1992 and 1995?

3. In October 1977 St Etienne were the visitors to Home Park for a European Cup-Winners' Cup tie. But who were the 'home' team?

## FRANCO BARESI

1. In his twenty-year career Baresi was a one-club man. But with which club?

2. At which Premier League club did he spend a short time with as Director of Football in 2002?

3. For which club did his brother Giuseppe make over 500 appearances between 1976 and 1992 – was it Inter Milan, Juventus or Roma?

## WHO'S MISSING – II

On April 15th 1967, Scotland came to Wembley to play England and famously beat the world champions 3-2. Below are eight of the Scottish line-up. Name the three missing players – one from Chelsea, one from Leeds and one from Man Utd.

Ronnie Simpson, Tommy Gemmell, \_\_\_?\_\_\_, John Greig, Ronnie McKinnon, Jim Baxter, William Wallace, \_\_\_?\_\_\_, Jim McCalliog, \_\_\_?\_\_\_, Bobby Lennox.

## SOME QUESTIONS ABOUT...
## GLASGOW RANGERS

1. Who was the catholic ex-Celtic striker controversially signed by Graeme Souness in 1989?

2. To date, Rangers have had fourteen managers since 1899. All have been Scottish born except for two. Name them.

3. In 1890/91, the inaugural season of the Scottish League, the championship was shared for the only time in its history. Rangers were one of the victorious teams. Who was the other – was it Queens Park, Dumbarton or Celtic?

## THE WORLD GAME – III

1.   Gunnar Gren, Gunnar Nordahl and Nils Liedholm formed a formidable strike-force for AC Milan during the 1950s, where they became known as 'Gre-No-Li'. For which country did they win a collective 111 caps?

2. Independiente of Argentina originally played in blue and white. But in 1907 their President witnessed an English team play in red shirts and consequently changed his own clubs colours to red. Which club was it?

3. Which two clubs contest 'El Clásico'?

## BENCHWARMING – I

**1986/87 was the last season where Football League clubs had the option of only one substitute. On the last Saturday of that season the following changes were made. Name the clubs that were playing each other.**

1. Jesper Olsen replaced Norman Whiteside and Stuart Ritchie replaced Andy Gray.

2. Keith Curle replaced Brian Williams and Chris Ramsey replaced Jimmy Quinn.

3. Mark Chamberlain replaced Mark Smith and Alan Cork replaced John Fashanu.

## SOME QUESTIONS ABOUT... HALIFAX TOWN

1. A tireless World Cup winner's father managed the club in two spells during the 60s and 70s. Name him.

2. In 1952/53 they welcomed Spurs to The Shay for an FA Cup 5th Round tie. What was the attendance – was it 17,399, 36,885 or 48,403?

3. In 2001/02, Halifax became the first Football League club to do what?

## THE 1960s – III

1. On August 21st 1965 Keith Peacock of Charlton became the first player to do what in a Football League match?

2. For their last three seasons in the Football League, Bradford PA finished bottom of Division 4. But where did they finish in 1966/67 – the season before this un-wanted hat-trick?

3. What were the managerial consequences for Ipswich when they won the Football League title in 1961/62?

## SIGN ON THE DOTTED LINE, SON – III

### Name the clubs that the following players first signed with as professionals.

1. David Platt.

2. Nigel Reo-Coker.

3. David Seaman.

## SOME QUESTIONS ABOUT...
## WEST HAM UNITED

1. What was the name of the club that the current West Ham was born out of in 1900 – was it Canning Town Wanderers, Thames Ironworks or Green Street Riveters?

2. Name two recent England centre-backs who spent time at West Ham's famous youth academy, but never graduated to their first-team?

3. A bronze statue of four 1966 World Cup winners stands close to Upton Park. Three are West Ham hero's Bobby Moore, Geoff Hurst and Martin Peters. Who is the fourth figure?

## THREE LIONS – III

1. Which former England caretaker won his four international caps whilst playing in Division 3, and which club was he playing for at the time?

2. Two England bosses managed the same club immediately before taking on the England job. Name them and the club?

3. Name the seven England managers who picked David Seaman to play in goal?

## STAT-TASTIC – III

**Identify the player from the following career statistics.**

Born: Dublin.
League Career Span: 1997/98 to the present.
International Caps: 81 apps – 33 goals (to date).

| CLUB/NICKNAME | LEAGUE APPS | GOALS |
|---|---|---|
| Wolves | 73 | 24 |
| Sky Blues | 31 | 12 |
| Nerazzurri | 6 | 0 |
| Peacocks (loan) | 18 | 9 |
| Peacocks | 28 | 4 |
| Spurs | 197 | 80 |
| Pool (to date) | 0 | 0 |

## SOME QUESTIONS ABOUT...
## FULCHESTER UNITED

1. What is the name of Fulchester's mullet-headed, fish-tailed goalkeeper?

2. What role did millionare pop-star Rick Spangle play at the club?

3. Ruthless millionaire Maxwell Baxter is frequently scheming to destroy Fulchester Utd. Who is the character primarily based on?

## IAN CALLAGHAN

1. What record does he hold for Liverpool?

2. Which former Liverpool player signed him in 1978, and for which club?

3. How many times was he booked during his career – was it once, forty-seven times or never?

## INTO THE LEAGUE! – II

### Guess the club from the details of their first ever home league game.

OPPOSITION: Burnley.
LEAGUE: Football League.
DATE: September 13th 1890.
HOME GROUND: Newcastle Road.
COLOURS: Red and white striped shirts, black knickers and stockings.

## SOME QUESTIONS ABOUT... FRANCE

1. Who captained France to the semi-final of the 1982 and 1986 World Cup – and who beat them on both occasions?

2. In hosting and winning Euro '84, France played five games in four different stadiums. They were Parc des Princes, La Beaujoire, Stade Geoffroy-Guichard and Stade Vélodrome. But which cities were they in?

3. In the 1958 World Cup finals, Just Fontaine scored a record 13 goals. Which two-time European Cup finalists did he play for at the time – was it Paris SG, AC Milan or Stade de Reims?

## PRE-1960s – III

1. In which year was the ban on women using Football Association members' pitches (instituted in 1921) lifted in England – was it 1953, 1971 or 1999?

2. When Albert Geldard made his debut for Bradford PA against Millwall in September 1929, how old was he – 47 years & 11 months, 13 years & 9 months or 15 years & 5 months?

3. In 1958 what did Everton install in an attempt to avoid postponements due to bad weather?

## 1966 AND ALL THAT... – II

1. Out of the 16 nations represented in the finals, name the four seeded teams.

2. The World Cup Final was played on Saturday July 30th. If the game had ended in a draw, when and where would the replay have been played?

3. Out of the eleven players who represented England in the World Cup Final, only two had played for more than one club at League level. Who were they and which clubs had they originally played for?

## SOME QUESTIONS ABOUT... MORECAMBE

1. Which manager gained his second promotion to the Football League when he took Morecambe up in 2006/07 – was it Jim Harvey, Sammy McIlroy or Brian Talbot?

2. In 2007/08 Christie Park had the seventh smallest capacity (6,400) in the Football League. Name the one Championship club who had a smaller capacity that season?

3. In both 2000/01 and 2002/03 non-league Morecambe reached the FA Cup 3rd Round. Which former East Anglian cup winners beat them on both occasions?

## EURO CHAMPIONSHIPS – III

1. Which two members of the England's Euro '88 squad were playing their club football for Monaco at the time?

2. Although they beat Germany 1-0, what were the results England suffered in their other two group games at Euro 2000, and who were they against?

3. What first occurred in the Euro '76 Final between Czechoslovakia and West Germany?

# HOW MUCH? – III

1. In 1999 Nicolas Anelka joined Real Madrid from Arsenal for a reported £22.5m. But how much did he cost the Gunners when he signed from Paris SG two years earlier – was it £0.5m, £2.5m or did he come on a free transfer?

2. Which then-Premier League club paid Celtic £4.7m for Paolo Di Canio in 1997?

3. To date only two players have broken the British transfer record twice. Both at their peak in the '60s and '70s, who are they?

## SOME QUESTIONS ABOUT...
## WEST BROMWICH ALBION

1. In 1969/70 they lost 2-1 to Man C in the League Cup Final at Wembley. Their next visit to the national stadium was twenty-three years later. What was the occasion?

2. In 1930/31 they won a unique 'double'. What was it?

3. Which player holds the record of most league appearances and goals (574 apps, 218 goals), most FA Cup appearances and goals (54 apps, 27 goals) and most European competition appearances and goals (17 apps, 8 goals) – is it Tony Brown, Cyrille Regis or Jeff Astle?

## TODAY'S THE DAY – III

**Identify the major news story that occurred on the day when the following events were happening in the world of football**

In their re-scheduled FA Cup 4th Round tie, a Peter Doherty-inspired Doncaster of Division 2 brush aside Division 1 Middlesbrough by 4-1 at Ayresome Park. Elsewhere in the cup two goals from Ronnie Allen are enough for WBA to see off Gateshead at St James' Park, and despite Jimmy Hill hitting the Luton post twice, Brentford have to settle for a goalless draw and a second replay at 'neutral' Highbury. It was noted that all players wore black armbands for their games.
Meanwhile at Sagana Lodge in Kenya...

## ME! ME! ME! – IV

### From the following description, guess who I am.

I was born in the east end but signed pro with north Londoners soon after the millennium. Lent to some birds of prey, I returned to establish myself as first choice. Two championships and three cup wins were tempered by a European final disappointment. But by this time I was seething at a derisory pay increase my club were offering. Some pensioners came tapping in an inappropriate manner for which we all got fined, but eventually I crossed over to the bridge. I've played for my country at European and world level and married a loud girl. We get by...

## SOME QUESTIONS ABOUT... CHELTENHAM TOWN

1. They won promotion to the Conference in 1996/97 and just two years later became a Football League club. Who was their manager during this period – was it Graham Allner, John Ward or Steve Cotterill?

2. 2008/09 sees Cheltenham's tenth season in the Football League. How many of those seasons have seen them play in the same division as Leyton Orient?

3. Which 'crazy' FA Cup winning manager was in charge for nine months in 2003?

## THE 2000s – IV

1. In 2005/06, which 'politicised' team began life in the North West Counties Football League Division 2 (level 10 of the English pyramid)?

2. Which manager and former Millers player took Rotherham to their second successive promotion in season 2000/01?

3. In winning the Premier League title in 2003/04, Arsenal went unbeaten. But how many of the 38 games did they draw – was it 9 games, 12 games or 16 games?

## REBRANDING TIME

**Club nicknames that were replaced, or never caught on.
Name the clubs that they belonged to.**

1. The Brewers.

2. The Dolphins.

3. The Oystermen.


## SOME QUESTIONS ABOUT... SOUTHAMPTON

1. Which future Spurs and England striker scored thirty goals as the Saints won promotion to Division 1 for the first time in 1965/66?

2. Between 1973 and 1985, they were led by Lawrie McMenemy. But which of the following players did not play under him – was it Alan Ball, Martin Peters, Charlie George, Peter Shilton, Kevin Keegan or Peter Osgood?

3. Following the demolition of The Dell, a housing estate was built on the site and the apartment blocks were named after Saints legends: Stokes Court, Bates Court, Le Tissier Court, Wallace Court and Channon Court. But what were these players' first names?


## WORLD CUP – IV

1. In the 2006 Final which ended 1-1 after extra time, the two goalscorers were involved in a major controversy. Who were they and what was the incident?

2. India qualified for the 1950 finals in Brazil, but withdrew before travelling. Why?

3. In which tournament was the current World Cup trophy first awarded to the winners?

## SKIPPER! – I

**Name the cup final, the year and the clubs involved
when the following captains led out their teams.**

1. Brian Kilcline and Richard Gough,

2. Billy McNeill and Armando Picchi,

3. Cafu and Oliver Kahn,

## SOME QUESTIONS ABOUT...
## STOCKPORT COUNTY

1. What was one of the major manufacturing industries in the area from which the club adopted their nickname?

2. Which manager became not only first Football League boss who did not speak English as a first language, but also the first manager born outside the British Isles to lead an English club out at Wembley?

3. In April 1982 Stockport suddenly changed their club colours. Why?

## BRIAN LABONE

1. Why did he withdraw from the 1966 England World Cup squad – was he injured, had he booked a holiday or was he getting married?

2. Complete this provocative Labone quote; "One ___?___ is worth twenty ___?___."

3. Who did he replace as centre-half for England in the 1970 World Cup finals?

## "YOU'LL NEVER TAKE THE HOME END!" – II

**A well-known 'Home End' – past or present.
Name the club it belongs to.**

1. Holte End.

2. London Road End.

3. Oak Road End.

## SOME QUESTIONS ABOUT...
## NEWPORT COUNTY

1. In 1946/47 they lost 13-0 in a Division 2 game. Len Shackleton, who was making his debut for the opposition and scored six of the goals, stated that Newport were "...lucky to get nil." Who were the opposition?

2. From 1979 to 1983 Newport had a prolific strike-force comprising of Tommy Tynan and which future Merseyside legend?

3. Which midfielder left Newport for Hereford in 1971 and proceeded to score the 'Goal Of The Season' in an FA Cup 3rd Round replay against Newcastle?

## THE 1990s – IV

1. When Burnley won the Division 4 title in 1991/92, they became only the second club to be champions of all four divisions. Who was the other club?

2. In 1993/94 which manager led Wycombe Wanderers to their second successive promotion as they won the Division 3 (4th tier) Play-Off Final?

3. Which two trophies did Arsene Wenger win in his debut season of 1997/98 at Arsenal?

## STRIKING FOR GLORY – IV

1. In 1975/76 Ted MacDougall, Derek Hales, 'Dixie' McNeil and Ronnie Moore were the top scorers in the four English divisions. Which clubs were they playing for?

2. Who are the top two all-time record goalscorers in the World Cup finals?

3. Which Sheff Utd striker scored the very first goal in the Premier League on August 15th 1992?

## SOME QUESTIONS ABOUT...
## BOLTON WANDERERS

1. Up to the end of 2007/08, how many seasons have Bolton spent in the top division – was it 47 seasons, 69 seasons or 99 seasons?

2. In 1987/88, which much decorated Liverpool full-back managed Bolton during their only season in Division 4?

3. Who was their last non-British manager?

## FA CUP – IV

1. In the 1932/33 final, what did the Everton and Man C teams wear for the first time in a major competitive game?

2. Between 1884 and 1886 Jimmy Brown became the first man to score in three consecutive finals – his club winning all three games. Who did he play for – Chelsea, Preston or Blackburn?

3. In 2003/04 Curtis Weston (Millwall) became the youngest player to appear in the final at the age of 17 years & 119 days. As a substitute, who did he replace with one minute of the match remaining?

## STARTING XI – III

**From this opening-day-of-the-season starting-eleven,
name the club and the season.**

Martyn, Kelly, Harte, Woodgate, Radebe, Bakke, Dacourt, Smith,
Bridges, Viduka, Bowyer.

# SOME QUESTIONS ABOUT... BAYERN MUNICH

1. Between 1974 and 1976, Sepp Maier, Hans-Georg Schwarzenbeck,
Franz Beckenbauer, Uli Hoeness and Gerd Müller played in all three
European Cup victories for Bayern. The same five players also appeared
for W. Germany in their Euro '72 victory, and their World Cup triumph of
1974. But one of the five missed the Germans defeat against
Czechoslovakia in Euro '76. Which one?

2. In August 2005 which Bayern midfielder became the first player to
score in a competitive match at their new Allianz Arena?

3. Which Frenchman won the World Cup whilst playing his club football
for Bayern – was it Zinedine Zidane, Bixente Lizarazu or Didier
Deschamps?

# A WORLD BEATING FOREIGN LEGION

Of the 14 players who won the World Cup for France in 1998, no less
than ten of them had played or would go on to play in the Premier
League. Name them and the clubs they played for.

## GETTING THERE – IV

**Arriving at the railway station, you jump in a cab. This is the route your taxi takes. But which ground are you heading to?**

It's about a mile and a half away. Take the first available left on to Western Esplanade. Follow Civic Centre Rd straight on and then in to New Road. Then follow the A3024 (Northam Rd) and take the third available right on to the B3038. Immediately turn right on to Britannia Rd and you're there.

## SOME QUESTIONS ABOUT... LINCOLN CITY

1. Who was manager in 1975/76 when they broke these records: most points for a season; most wins and fewest defeats; first club in nearly a decade to score over 100 league goals?

2. Between 2002/03 and 2006/07, how many times did Lincoln contest the play-offs?

3. In 1976, which future European Cup winning England striker played six games on loan from Nott'm Forest?

## THE 1980s – IV

1. In 1984/85, which two clubs contested the League Cup Final but also got relegated from Division 1?

2. In 1988/89, two west-midlands clubs fell into Division 3 – one of them for the first time. Who were they?

3. Who did John Docherty succeed as Millwall manager in July 1986?

## HOW MUCH? – IV

1. In May 2006, goalkeeper Joe Hart joined Man C for an initial fee of £600,000. But from which club?

2. Which Italian side did John Charles join when he left Leeds for £65,000 in 1957?

3. Between Kevin Keegan's £0.5m transfer in 1977, and Trevor Francis' reputed £1m transfer in February 1979, who held the record as England's most expensive player when he left Middlesbrough for WBA in January 1979?

## SOME QUESTIONS ABOUT... COVENTRY CITY

1. They were founded as Singers FC in 1883. What did Singers manufacture – was it bicycles, mangles or sewing machines?

2. What sartorial change did Jimmy Hill make when he became manager in 1961?

3. In 2000/01 Coventry were relegated from the Premier League. But how many consecutive seasons had they survived in the top division?

## HOME OF THE BRAVE – IV

1. Livingston FC have had two previous incarnations. Name them.

2. Between 1985/86 and 2007/08, how many clubs outside the 'Old Firm' won the Scottish title?

3. In eight World Cup final tournaments, how many times have Scotland progressed beyond the first round of matches?

## SEQUENCES – IV

### Who is next in the following sequences?

1. East Stirling, East Stirling, East Stirling, ___?___.

2. Don Revie, Brian Clough, Jimmy Armfield, ___?___.

3. Uruguay, Italy, Italy, ___?___.

## SOME QUESTIONS ABOUT...
## SCUNTHORPE UNITED

1. When they moved from the Old Show Ground to Glanford Park, they became the first English club in the modern era to relocate to a new purpose-built stadium. What year was it?

2. In 2007/08 which versatile defender and son of a prominent member of 'The Crazy Gang', played 34 games whilst on loan from Chelsea?

3. Name the three ex-Scunthorpe players who have captained England?

## EUROPEAN SILVERWARE – IV

1. In 1985 three Italians – Gaetano Scirea, Antonio Cabrini and Marco Tardelli – became the first players to hold winners medals for all three major European trophies with the same team. Which team was it?

2. In the 2008 Champions League Final which player from Man Utd and which from Chelsea took the first penalties in the shoot-out?

3. To date, five British clubs have been losing finalists in the European Cup/Champions League Final. Name them.

## THE BIG JOB – II

### Who had the full-time managers job either side of the following appointments?

1. West Ham: ___?___ (1961-74) John Lyall (1974-89) ___?___ (1989-90)

2. Derby: ___?___ (1984) Arthur Cox (1984-93) ___?___ (1993-95)

3. Aston Villa: ___?___ (1987-90) Jozef Venglos (1990-91) ___?___ (1991-94)

## SOME QUESTIONS ABOUT... TURKEY

1. In the 2002 World Cup tournament, which country did they lose to in both the group stage and the semi-final?

2. Turkey have given caps to two English-born players since 2000. Name them.

3. There was only one player who contested both the 2002 World Cup semi-final and Euro 2008 semi-final. Was it Rustu Recbar, Hakan Sukar or Hasan Sas?

## THE 1970s – IV

1. In 1974, when Brian Clough was sacked from Leeds, assistant manager Maurice Lindsey, chief coach Syd Owen and one senior player picked the team for the next game. Who was that player?

2. Within four seasons both Watford and Swansea would be in the top division. But in 1978/79 they finished second and third respectively to which Shropshire team who eclipsed them both to the Division 3 title?

3. The teams that occupied the top five positions in Division 4 in 1972/73 had all lost their league status by season 2005/06. Name them.

# BY MUTUAL CONSENT? – IV

**Identify the well-known manager from the following clues.**

Born by the Clyde, he was known for controversy rather than trophy-winning. The majority of his playing career was with north enders and gunners though he had spells with bhoys and pensioners. It was with old folk that he had his first managerial role, leading them to domestic cup triumph and failure. Spells with millers, bush people, villans and Iberian dragons led to the national job. But the opportunity to boss the biggest club in Britain was too good to refuse. Although in transition, he got them on their feet and ended with a cup that had eluded him – and a liaison that brought him the sack. Interspersed with periods down-under, he bossed quadruped livestock, bushmen (again), north enders and old gold midlanders, before finishing with non-league Cheshire robins.

# SOME QUESTIONS ABOUT... SHREWSBURY TOWN

1. When the Football League expanded from 88 to 92 clubs in 1950/51, Shrewsbury were one of the four teams admitted. Name the other three.

2. What connects Town to Mr Burns, Smithers and Ned Flanders?

3. In 1961 Arthur Rowley scored his 380th league goal in a game against Bradford C. Which Everton legend held the record prior to this?

# THE WORLD GAME – IV

1. Which chain-smoking World Cup winning boss briefly managed Mexico in the early 1990s?

2. Cesare Maldini, Dino Zoff, Giovanni Trapattoni, Marcello Lippi and Roberto Donadoni. They have all managed Italy, but who is the odd-one out on two counts, and why?

3. The so-called 'Football War' of 1969 involved which two neighbouring Central American countries?

## ... WAIT A MINUTE MR POSTMAN! – I

### Identify the stadium and the clubs that play at these postal locations.

1. L_____ S_____, Landore, SA1 2FA

2. K_ S_____, The Circle, Walton St, Anlaby Rd, HU3 6HU

3. C___ o_ M_____ S_____, SportCity, M11 3FF

## SOME QUESTIONS ABOUT... SHEFFIELD WEDNESDAY

1. Why are they known as 'The Owls'?

2. Wednesday have had three bosses who have also managed at international level. Name them and the countries they managed.

3. In the 1965/66 FA Cup Final against Everton, Wednesday won the toss to decide who would wear their regular strip of blue and white. However, Wednesday decided to play in their 'away' strip of all white. Why?

## PETER SCHMEICHEL

1. Though born in Denmark, Schmeichel only became a Danish citizen in 1970. Where was his father born – was it Austria, Poland or Switzerland?

2. How many Premier League titles did he win with Man Utd?

3. Whilst playing for Aston Villa in 2001, Schmeichel became the first goalkeeper to score a Premier League goal. Name the other two goalkeepers who have since achieved this feat.

## SIGN ON THE DOTTED LINE, SON – IV

**Name the clubs that the following players
first signed with as professionals.**

1. Marcus Bent.

2. Billy Bonds.

3. Andy Cole.

## SOME QUESTIONS ABOUT... BRAZIL

1. In the 1954 World Cup quarter-final, who were their opponents in the infamous 'Battle of Berne'?

2. Which one of the following players appeared in the 1970 World Cup Final against Italy, but didn't play when they opened their defence of the trophy against Yugoslavia four years later; Piazza, Jairzinho, Rivelino or Gerson?

3. In their final group match at the 1958 World Cup, Brazil faced the much-fancied USSR. Senior players suggested three changes to counter the expected threat. One player brought in for his World Cup debut was Zito. Who were the other two?

## THE 1960s – IV

1. Which East London club finished bottom of Division 1 at the end of 1962/63?

2. In 1967/68 which club was relegated to Division 4 after having 19 points deducted for illegal payments to players – was it Luton, Peterborough or Rochdale?

3. In 1964/65, which club completed its five-year journey, which involved three promotions, from Division 4 to Division 1?

## WHAT'S THAT ON THE FRONT
## OF YOUR SHIRT? – I

**These are selected shirt sponsors over the years.
Name the club.**

1. 'Loaded' – 'Maximuscle' – 'PopVase.com'

2. 'Top Man' – 'Admiral' – 'Packard Bell'

3. 'Avco' – 'Dagenham Motors' – 'Dr Martens'

## SOME QUESTIONS ABOUT... SWANSEA CITY

1. Roberto Martinez became Swans boss in 2007. But he first came to England from Spain in 1995 with compatriots Jesús Seba and Isidro Díaz. Which club did the 'three amigos' join?

2. Which young West Ham midfielder played nine games on loan to the Swans in the mid '90s?

3. What do ex-Swansea strikers Leon Knight and Bob Latchford have in common?

## THREE LIONS – IV

1. Which one of the following players was a 'One-Cap-Wonder' – was it Frank Lampard Snr, Brian Clough or Charlie George?

2. How old was Stanley Matthews when he scored his last goal for England against N. Ireland on October 10th 1956 – 37 years & 3 months, 45 years & one week or 41 years & 8 months?

3. Which organisation did England join in 1906, leave in 1928, and re-join in 1946?

## STAT-TASTIC – IV

**Identify the player from the following career statistics.**

Born: Aberdeen.
League Career Span: 1956/57 to 1973/74.
International Caps: 55 apps – 30 goals.

| CLUB/NICKNAME | LEAGUE APPS | GOALS |
|---|---|---|
| Terriers | 81 | 16 |
| Citizens | 44 | 21 |
| Granata | 27 | 10 |
| Red Devils | 309 | 171 |
| Citizens | 24 | 9 |

# SOME QUESTIONS ABOUT... BOURNEMOUTH

1. In the early 1970s they were 're-branded' as the continental sounding AFC Bournemouth. What were they known as before?

2. In 2003/04, James Hayter scored the fastest hat trick in Football League history in a match against Wrexham. How long did it take – 1 mins 47 secs, 3 mins 14 secs or 2 mins 20 secs?

3. On May 7th 1983, which player turned out for his very last league game in a Division 3 fixture against Wigan?

## CARLOS TEVEZ

1. Diego Maradona once described Tevez as what?
a) "The Argentine prophet for the 21st century."
b) "The most naturally gifted player since myself."
c) "Overrated."

2. On May 13th 2007, Tévez secured West Ham's Premier League status by scoring the only goal in a 1-0 victory. Who was it against?

3. Which Brazilian club did he and his compatriot Javier Mascherano play for before signing for West Ham in August 2006?

## OLD GROUNDS FOR NEW – II

### Which clubs used to play their home games at the following grounds?

1. Loakes Park.

2. Huish.

3. Plough Lane.


## SOME QUESTIONS ABOUT... BARCELONA

1. Apart from Barca, which two other clubs have never been relegated from La Liga since its formation in 1928?

2. Which of the following Dutchmen has, to date, never managed Barca – Rinus Michels, Johan Cruyff, Leo Beenhakker, Louis Van Gaal or Frank Rijkaard?

3. In 1973/74 Dutch legend Johan Cruyff stated why he chose to join Barca rather than Real Madrid. Which one was it?
a) He could never play for a club associated with General Franco
b) He preferred Barcelona's colours.
c) He was a personal friend of Barca manager Rinus Michels.


## PRE-1960s – IV

1. Which World Cup winner made his debut on April 25th 1953, in a Division 2 Yorkshire derby?

2. Which club held the Football League title throughout both World Wars?

3. In the ten seasons between 1949/50 and 1958/59, Wolves and Man Utd won the Football League title three times each. Which four teams won the other titles?

# EURO '96 AND ALL THAT – II

1. Who scored the first goal of the tournament?

2. Who equalised Alan Shearer's opening goal in the semi-final between England and Germany?

3. Six nations were making their Euro Championship debuts. Name them.

# SOME QUESTIONS ABOUT... BARNET

1. In 1978/79, which prolific English striker scored 25 goals for the then Southern League outfit?

2. Between 1985 and 1993, who was their controversial chairman, and allegedly, what did he do regularly to manager Barry Fry?

3. In their first Football League game in 1991/92, the Bees opened with a 7-4 defeat at home to Crewe. They then met Brentford in a League Cup 1st Round tie. What was the score – was it 8-2, 1-9 or was it a 5-5 draw?

# EURO CHAMPIONSHIPS – IV

1. The 1968 semi-final between Italy and USSR ended 0-0 after extra time. How was the match decided?

2. The USSR had already qualified for the 1992 finals, but the country was in the process of breaking-up into independent states. Under what title did they travel to the tournament in Sweden?

3. In the two-legged quarter-finals of Euro '60, which country – then living under a nationalist dictatorship – refused to travel to the Soviet Union for their away leg, and were subsequently eliminated from the tournament?

# ODD ONE OUT – II

### From this list, name the one league club
### that Frank Worthington did not play for.

Huddersfield, Leicester, Bolton, Birmingham, Everton, Leeds, Sunderland, Southampton, Brighton, Tranmere, Preston and Stockport.

# SOME QUESTIONS ABOUT... WATFORD

1. In 1987 which manager, with a knack of getting the best out of limited resources, took over when Graham Taylor left for Aston Villa?

2. Which single player has appeared and scored most times for Watford?

3. In 1988/89 who kept goal for their FA Youth Cup winning team?

# TODAY'S THE DAY – IV

### Identify the major news story that occurred on the day when
### the following events were happening in the world of football.

In Belfast, a Derek Dougan goal is scant consolation for N. Ireland as they are thrashed 5-1 by Wales. In the European Cup semi-final, Barcelona will take a 1-0 lead into the second leg against Hamburg. On the domestic front Man Utd inflict a 6-0 defeat on Football League Champions and current high-flyers Burnley, with two goals apiece from Albert Quixall and Denis Violett. In Scotland however, Morton's Division 2 game against Queens Park is postponed due to a waterlogged pitch. Meanwhile 189 miles above the earth...

## ME! ME! ME! – V

### From the following description, guess who I am.

I achieved over 100 caps plus both major international trophies. I started locally with blue gods and then with reds. Then it was time to explore a bit of Europe, with stints at Lombardy's fashion capital, followed by a sovereign city-state on the north coast of the Med. I then joined riding-boot accessories in the capital where I successfully overcame deep-rooted national prejudice – even going back there for a second spell. I moved on to Bavarian reds and Blue-ringed Genoans before wrapping-up my playing career across the pond with a citrus-flavoured blue luminous ball of plasma. I have managed my country and my home country's most famous club.

## SOME QUESTIONS ABOUT... CHESTER CITY

1. At the beginning of 1974/75, Chester were the only Football League club left to achieve what?

2. Between 1990 and 1992, which ground did they use for 'home' games whilst the Deva Stadium was being built?

3. In their epic League Cup run of 1974/75, the father of which future England international striker scored Chester's opening goal in the semi-final 1st leg against Aston Villa?

## THE 2000s – V

1. In July 2002 Leicester City moved into their new home, The Walkers Stadium. But when the crisp manufacturer bought the naming rights, what were they originally going to call it?

2. Which home ground did Colchester leave at the end of 2007/08?

3. In 2006 Niall Quinn led a consortium that took control of Sunderland. He became chairman and, briefly, manager. Name the only other league club who could boast a chairman/manager at that time?

## THEME CHOONS

### Which clubs traditionally take the field to the following tunes?

1. The Post Horn Gallop.

2. The theme from 'Z' Cars.

3. Glad All Over.

## SOME QUESTIONS ABOUT...
## HUDDERSFIELD TOWN

1. In December 1957 Huddersfield travelled to Charlton for a Division 2 game. Town led 5-1 with 30 minutes left and their opponents down to ten men. What was the final score – was it 7-6 to Charlton, 6-5 to Huddersfield or was it a 6-6 draw?

2. Whose £55,000 transfer to Man C in 1961 financed the instillation of floodlights at Leeds Rd?

3. Huddersfield won two of their three consecutive Football League titles under Herbert Chapman. But which club did he join after the second success in 1924/25?

## WORLD CUP – V

1. Italy have generally played in azure blue shirts. But what colour did they wear for the 1938 World Cup tournament held in France?

2. What did Mordechai Spiegler achieve for Israel against Sweden in a 1970 Group Two game?

3. In the 1962 tournament the host nation, Chile, allegedly ate Swiss cheese before beating Switzerland, spaghetti before defeating Italy and drank Vodka before their victory against the USSR. What were they rumoured to have drunk prior to their semi-final against Brazil?

## HE SAID WHAT? – IV

### Who are responsible for these quotes?

1. "When I heard Jonathan repeat the figure of £55K, I nearly swerved off the road. 'He's taking the piss, Jonathan!' I yelled down the phone. I was so incensed. I was trembling with anger. I couldn't believe what I'd heard. I suppose it all started to fall apart for me from then on."

2. "There'll never be a soccer player like Pelé. Better than Pelé, maybe, but not like Pelé."

3. "Lamps is Lamps. When he plays well he is best in the game. When he plays bad, he is the second or the third best."

## SOME QUESTIONS ABOUT... GRIMSBY TOWN

1. Which manager joined them from Doncaster in 1971 and led them to the Division 4 title in his first season?

2. Which future England manager made his league debut in a 2-1 victory over Newcastle in September 1963?

3. In 1976, the then American Secretary of State for the USA witnessed a game at Blundell Park against Gillingham. Was it Cyrus Vance, Jimmy Carter or Dr Henry Kissinger?

## STEVE BRUCE

1. Which future England international travelled with Bruce to Gillingham for a trial – and was rejected?

2. What did Bruce do in the first minute of his debut for Norwich against Liverpool in 1984?

3. Name the five league clubs he has managed to date.

# WHO'S MISSING? – III

**Below are eight of the Wimbledon starting line-up
who beat Liverpool in the 1988 FA Cup Final.
Name the three missing players.**

Dave Beasant, Clive Goodyear, ___?___, Vinny Jones, Eric Young, Andy Thorn, Terry Gibson, ___?___, John Fashanu, Lawrie Sanchez, ___?___.

# SOME QUESTIONS ABOUT... ARSENAL

1. In which area of London is the Emirates Stadium based – is it Finsbury Park, Holloway or Islington and Canonbury?

2. In 2005/06, Arsenal lost to Barcelona in the Champions League Final. But prior to this, who were the last London club to contest a major European final?

3. When club physiotherapist Bertie Mee was surprisingly appointed as manager in 1966, he appointed a right-hand-man who would soon move on to take over at Chelsea. Name him.

# THE 1990s – V

1. In November 1990 Colin Harvey was sacked as Everton manager. But what was his next job?

2. In December 1994 what did Colchester lose and local rivals Ipswich gain?

3. On May 14th 2000, Wimbledon were relegated from the Premier League after 14 years in the top flight. But what had they achieved on the very same date twelve years previously?

## STRIKING FOR GLORY – V

1. Which Brazilian is the only player to score in every game played by his country at a single World Cup tournament – including the final?

2. In 1937/38 how many goals did Raith score in their 38 game journey to the Scottish Division 2 title – was it 42, 142 or 166?

3. Twice during 2007/08 Reading scored four goals, but still lost. Who were these games against and what were the final scores?

## SOME QUESTIONS ABOUT... HAMILTON ACADEMICAL

1. In 1971 the Accies signed three Polish players – Witold Szygula, Roman Strazalkowski and Alfred Olek. What was significant about this?

2. Two Scottish international keepers, with almost 100 caps between them, spent the briefest of times at Hamilton during their careers. Name them.

3. Who played a handful of games for the Accies in 1993/94, before signing for Preston and eventually becoming a Merseyside boss?

## FA CUP – V

1. Which team got knocked out of the 1999/2000 FA Cup twice, and why?

2. The 1979/80 semi-final between Arsenal and Liverpool was played at Hillsborough. The first and second replays were at Villa Park. But where was the third and final replay played – was it Highfield Road, Burnden Park or Bramall Lane?

3. In 1887, Preston beat Hyde in a 1st Round game by a score that remains a record to this day. What was it?

## WHAT'S IN A NICKNAME? – II

### Guess the club from this description of their nickname.

This Society of Friends was founded in England during the 17th century. They distance themselves from creeds and hierarchical structure, and they meet without any formal ceremony or leader.

## SOME QUESTIONS ABOUT... BARROW

1. In 1958/59 Barrow were drawn against the Football League Champions in the FA Cup 3rd Round. They lost 4-2, but who were their opponents?

2. Which teenage European Cup winner was manager for a short period in 1984/85?

3. At the end of 1971/72 Barrow lost their Football League status. How did this happen – were they relegated, did they go bankrupt and resign from the Football League or were they voted out?

## SURNAMES

### What surnames to the following players share?

1. Andy, Joe, Ashley.

2. Cliff, Joey, Vinnie.

3. Les, Anton, Rio.

## GETTING THERE – V

**Arriving at the railway station, you jump in a cab. This is the route your taxi takes. But which ground are you heading to?**

It's just over a mile away. Head northwest and turn left into Station Rd. At the roundabout, take the second exit onto the High St. At Isaac's Hill Roundabout, take the second exit onto the A180. Just keep going and eventually turn right into Constitutional Ave and you're there.

## SOME QUESTIONS ABOUT... SWINDON TOWN

1. In August 1920, in their very first Football League game, they recorded their record victory against Luton. What was the score – was it 9-1, 11-0 or 14-4?

2. When, as a Division 3 club, they beat Arsenal to win the 1968/69 League Cup, they should have gone on to play in the Inter-Cities Fairs Cup the following season. Why didn't they?

3. Which World Cup winner took over as manager from Lou Macari in 1989?

## THE 1980s – V

1. Which former European Cup-Winners' Cup quarter-finalists lost their Football League status in 1987/88?

2. Which two clubs from the same city finished as Division 3 champions and runner-up in 1989/90?

3. In 1983/84, which club narrowly escaped relegation to Division 4, but reached the FA Cup semi-final?

# THAT'S MY BOY! – I

**What were the first management jobs for these father and sons?**

1. Alex and Darren Ferguson.

2. Brian and Nigel Clough.

3. Alan Ball Snr and Alan Ball Jnr.

# SOME QUESTIONS ABOUT...
# NOTTINGHAM FOREST

1. In the late 19th century, which club did they donate a set of red jerseys to?

2. Between 1975 and 1996, Forest had only two managers. Name them.

3. Which two clubs did they beat to win their two European Cups in 1978/79 and 1979/80?

# HOME OF THE BRAVE – V

1. When Celtic won the 1966/67 Scottish League title, they lost just two games – both to the same team. Was it Cowdenbeath, Third Lanark or Dundee Utd?

2. In the late 1990s whilst Hampden Park was being refurbished, five other stadiums were used for World Cup and Euro Championship qualifying games by the national team. Name them.

3. In the fifty years since 1957/58, name the five clubs other than Celtic and Rangers who have carried off the Scottish Championship?

## SEQUENCES – V

### Who is next in the following sequences?

1. Carlos Alberto Parreira, Aime Jacquet, Luiz Felipe Scolari, ___?___.

2. Plough Lane, Selhurst Park, The National Hockey Stadium, ___?___.

3. Joe Royle, Kevin Keegan, Stuart Pearce, ___?___.

## SOME QUESTIONS ABOUT... GERMANY

1. When was the last time that Germany lost a penalty shoot-out in a major tournament?

2. In Euro '96 Andreas Möller scored the decisive penalty in a semi-final shoot-out against England. In the 2002 World Cup semi-final Michael Ballack scored the only goal. What happened to both players in the respective finals?

3. In 1950, and under Allied occupation, three separate 'national' teams within German boundaries were recognised by FIFA. Name them.

## EUROPEAN SILVERWARE – V

1. Which London team contested the first Inter-Cities Fairs Cup Final against Barcelona in 1958 – was it a London XI, Chelsea or Spurs?

2. In 1998/99 Dutch Cup semi-finalists SC Heerenveen became the only club to enter the European Cup-Winners' Cup competition despite not having contested their own domestic cup final. How did this come about?

3. Name the ten full England internationals that played in the Champions League Final of 2008?

## ANOTHER BITE AT THE CHERRY? – III

Which five Leeds players lost to Liverpool in the 1964/65 FA Cup Final, but returned to Wembley seven years later to lift the trophy with victory over Arsenal?

## SOME QUESTIONS ABOUT... MAIDSTONE UNITED

1. In which town did the play their 'home' games during a very brief Football League life – was it in Dartford, Thurrock or Gillingham?

2. Which TV pundit's father managed them during their first Football League season of 1989/90?

3. Another Football League club went out of business in 1992. Name them.

## THE 1970s – V

1. Which East Anglian club gained promotion to the top flight for the first time at the end of season 1971/72?

2. In 1979, and after over twenty years of service, Alan Hardaker passed on the job of Secretary of the Football League to a new man. Was it Bert Millichip, Ken Bates or Graham Kelly?

3. In December 1979, which goalkeeping legend was sacked as reserve team coach at Port Vale?

## BY MUTUAL CONSENT? – V

### Identify the well-known manager from the following clues.

This son of a Lombardy industrialist began his career with a local club where his striking abilities were recognised by Genoans and then by an old lady. He won scudetto with both these sides whilst becoming one of the greatest goal scorers in his country's history. Shortly after leading his club to European glory a new challenge beckoned – this time with rejuvenating old men in SW6 where he became a favourite. The departure of a Dutch master saw him take over and he swiftly provided both domestic and European silverware while still hitting the target regularly. A surprise sacking led him to a vicarage where he expensively failed in an attempt to lead them back to the 'promised land'. He was more recently linked with driven, moneyed bushmen, but declined any interest in the hot seat.

## SOME QUESTIONS ABOUT... BURNLEY

1. Which club inspired their change of kit from green to claret and blue in 1910/11?

2. England settled on Alf Ramsey as new manager in 1963. But which Burnley player and coach was initially approached for the job by the FA?

3. The East Lancashire 'derby' is contested between Burnley and Blackburn. But which Football League club lies geographically between the two?

## SLAVEN BILIC

1. Who signed him for West Ham in 1996?

2. Which other English club did he play for?

3. He was appointed Croatia's manager in 2006. But who was he in charge of prior to this?

## HOW MUCH? – V

1. In 1971 which England World Cup winner became the most expensive English transfer at £220,000 – and whose record transfer did his beat?

2. Which Hackney-born striker has, to date, totalled transfers of just under £16m over his fifteen-year career?

3. Hernán Crespo joined Lazio in 2000 for £35.5m, and Gianluigi Buffon went to Juventus for £32.6m 2001. In both cases who was the selling club?

## SOME QUESTIONS ABOUT...
## DONCASTER ROVERS

1. In 1995, chairman Ken Richardson found a novel way of trying to pay off the clubs debts. What was it?

2. Harry Gregg became the worlds most expensive goalkeeper when he left Doncaster for £23,500 in 1957. Who did he join?

3. Not only did Charlie Williams play over 150 games at centre-half for Doncaster, he was also one of Britain's first well-known black stand-up comedians. But what popular 1970s TV series made him famous?

## THE WORLD GAME – V

1. Which shirt number did Ajax retire in 2007/08, and why?

2. Spanish club Villarreal have the nickname of a colourful Beatles song. What is it?

3. In 1977/78 Borussia Mönchengladbach beat Borussia Dortmund 12-0. The Dortmund coach was immediately sacked but went on to lead a nation to Euro Championship glory. Was it Berti Vogts, Otto Rehhagel or Richard Møller Nielsen?

## SIGN ON THE DOTTED LINE, SON – V

### Name the clubs that the following players first signed with as professionals.

1. Craig Bellamy.

2. Tony Currie.

3. Jamie Redknapp.


## SOME QUESTIONS ABOUT... ARGENTINA

1. Which one of the following did not play in both the 1986 and 1990 World Cup Final's against Germany; Sergio Goycochea, Jorge Burruchaga, Diego Maradona or Oscar Ruggeri?

2. In July 2007 which former Premier League striker scored in Argentina's 4-2 victory over Colombia, and in doing so overhauled Diego Maradona's tally of 34 international goals?

3. Winner of five European Cup titles with Real Madrid, Alfredo di Stefano played international football for two other countries apart from Argentina. Name them.


## THE 1960s – V

1. Which two clubs from the same city finished Football League champions and runners-up in 1967/68 – and in what order did they finish?

2. Which no-nonsense Liverpool full-back made his league debut on the last day of 1962/63 in a comprehensive 5-1 victory over Birmingham at Anfield?

3. Which two West London clubs finished bottom of Division 1 and Division 2 in 1968/69?

## STARTING XI – IV

**From this opening-day-of-the-season starting-eleven,
name the club and the season.**

Green, Webster, Robson, Durban, McFarland, Mackay, McGovern, Carlin, O'Hare, Hector, Hinton.

## SOME QUESTIONS ABOUT... LEEDS UNITED

1. Following the appointment of Don Revie in 1961, a struggling and unhappy defender almost left to join Man Utd. Who was it?

2. There are three players that played under Don Revie who would later become Leeds bosses themselves. Name them.

3. In 1974, Brian Clough was famously manager for only 44 days. In 1978 how long did Jock Stein last?

## THREE LIONS – V

1. How many occasions did both Billy Wright and Bobby Moore captain England – was it 57 times, 73 times or 90 times?

2. In March 1923 Belgium became England's first continental opposition on home soil. On which London ground was the game played?

3. Which two former England managers were born in Lancashire?

## STAT-TASTIC – V

### Identify the player from the following career statistics.

Born: Archway, London.
League Career Span: 1974/75 to 1988/89.
International Caps: 6 apps – 0 goals.

| CLUB/NICKNAME | LEAGUE APPS | GOALS |
| --- | --- | --- |
| O's | 75 | 15 |
| Baggies | 86 | 21 |
| Los Blancos | 44 | 13 |
| Red Devils (loan) | 5 | 1 |
| Rojiblancos | 30 | 3 |
| l'OM | 30 | 8 |
| Foxes | 15 | 0 |
| Rayo | 37 | 3 |
| Les Zèbres | 1 | 0 |
| Crazy Gang | 6 | 2 |
| Rayo | 19 | 1 |

## SOME QUESTIONS ABOUT...
## MILTON KEYNES DONS

1. Which three clubs did Pete Winkelman approach about moving to Milton Keynes before 'finding' Wimbledon?

2. Where did they play their 'home' games until 2006/07?

3. On August 2nd 2007, what did MK Dons return to the London Borough of Merton?

## LIAM BRADY

1. Which league club did he finish his playing career with?

2. Which Frenchman's arrival was instrumental in Brady moving from Juventus to Sampdoria in 1982?

3. At Arsenal, he was nicknamed 'Chippy'. Why?

## ... WAIT A MINUTE MR POSTMAN! – II

### Identify the stadium and the clubs that play at these postal locations.

1. K_____ S_____, Stadium Way, Lakeside, DN4 5JW

2. M_____ S_____, Filton Avenue, Horfield, BS7 0BF

3. A_____ P___, Hillbottom Rd, Sands, HP12 4HJ

## SOME QUESTIONS ABOUT... LUTON TOWN

1. Which future Luton and Spurs manager played in the Division 4 title team of 1967/68?

2. In the final game of 1982/83 Luton beat Man C at Maine Rd to ensure their Division 1 survival and the relegation of their opponents. But which Yugoslav defender, who would go on to manage Real Madrid and Barcelona, scored the decisive goal four minutes from time?

3. In 1935/36, Luton beat Bristol R 12-0. How many goals did stand-in striker Joe Payne score?

## PRE-1960s – V

1. In 1952/53 who won the West German championship – a feat they would not repeat until 1990/91 – was it Schalke 04, Hamburg or Kaiserslautern?

2. Which striker scored a record 34 hat-tricks in his career for Tranmere, Everton, Notts Co and England?

3. Which record breaking defensive wing-half retired with a championship medal at the end of 1958/59?

## 1966 AND ALL THAT... – III

1. Name the eight stadiums used during the tournament?

2. Before 1966 which two previous hosts had won the tournament?

3. Why was the Group One game between Uruguay and France switched from Wembley Stadium to the White City Stadium?

## SOME QUESTIONS ABOUT... TORQUAY UNITED

1. In 1963 Torquay signed striker Robin Stubbs. In 238 appearances he would score 121 goals. But what connected him to 'Mr Entertainment' Bruce Forsyth?

2. Frank O'Farrell became boss in 1965 and recruited former teammates John Bond and Ken Brown. Both would soon become respected managers in their own right. But from which club did O'Farrell sign them?

3. In 1991/92 Torquay were relegated from Division 3. But they began the following season still in the Division 3. How?

## EURO CHAMPIONSHIPS – V

1. Of the four games that Portugal played in Euro '84, Manuel Jordao was the only player making an appearance who didn't play his club football for Benfica or Porto. Who did he play for – was it Sporting Lisbon, Vitória Setúbal or Portimonense?

2. Germany have contested the most actual Finals, with six appearances. But which nation comes next having appeared in four Finals?

3. Which Belgian stadium hosted the 1972 Final between W. Germany and USSR?

## "YOU'LL NEVER TAKE THE HOME END!" – III

### A well-known 'Home End' – past or present.
### Name the club it belongs to.

1. Kippax.

2. The Shed.

3. The Loft.

## SOME QUESTIONS ABOUT... LEYTON ORIENT

1. Which player who started his career at Brisbane Rd, went to Spain and won La Liga and Copa del Rey before returning home for an FA Cup winners medal?

2. Having been Clapton Orient from 1898, they became Leyton Orient in 1946... and again in 1987. But what were they called between 1966 and 1987?

3. In 1930/31, having had to vacate their home ground, they played two Division 3 (South) games at a suburban London venue. Which one?

## TODAY'S THE DAY – V

### Identify the major news story that occurred on the day when the following events were happening in the world of football

Brian Clough is awarded Nottingham's 'Citizen of the Month' for talking an epileptic alcoholic out of jumping from a bridge into the River Trent. Two goals from Mark Hateley in a 5-0 victory over Watford help Coventry to progress to the League Cup semi-finals, and Neville Southall is denied his first major honour as Bury can only draw with Chesterfield (losing 3-2 on aggregate) in the semi-final of the Anglo-Scottish Cup. Meanwhile outside The Dakota apartment building in New York...

## ME! ME! ME! – VI

### From the following description, guess who I am.

I was brought up in a tough capital district but began my career as a winger under my future-mentor in a southern tax haven. An old lady took me to an unsettled time in car-manufacturing Piedmont, and I soon re-joined my mentor at capital gunmen where I added some va-va voom to my game and struck with regularity. Domestic and personal honours came in abundance. I broke individual scoring records, though European trophies would elude me. Eventually it was time to move on, and I became Catalan. On the international stage I warmed the bench for my country's greatest moment but played my part two years later to win Europe's top prize.

## SOME QUESTIONS ABOUT... JUVENTUS

1. What is the 'Derby della Mole'?

2. In 1903 Juventus turned to an English player for help in getting some new kit. John Savage wrote to a friend back home, and a delivery of black and white striped shirts duly arrived. But in which city was this friend based?

3. Which one of the following Italian national team bosses never managed Juventus – Cesare Maldini, Dino Zoff, Giovanni Trapattoni and Marcello Lippi?

## THE 2000s – VI

1. Following promotion from the Conference, which two clubs began their very first season in the Football League in 2007/08?

2. On April 10th 2005 which striker became the youngest goalscorer to-date in the history of the Premier League?

3. In 2003/04 two newly promoted midland clubs to the Premier League went straight back down to Division 1 (2nd tier) Who were they?

## BENCHWARMING – II

**The following substitutions were made in FA Cup finals.
Name the year and the clubs that were playing each other.**

1. Eddie Kelly replaced Peter Storey and Peter Thompson replaced Alun Evans.

2. David McCreery replaced Gordon Hill and Ian Callaghan replaced David Johnson

3. Mick Lambert replaced Roger Osborne and Graham Rix replaced Liam Brady

## SOME QUESTIONS ABOUT... CHESTERFIELD

1. Which Scottish international goalkeeper, who won a coveted league and cup 'double', was born in Chesterfield but never played for them?

2. Who did they lose to after a replay in the 1996/97 FA Cup Semi-Final – was it Chelsea, Newcastle or Middlesbrough?

3. The Spireites are recognised as the fourth oldest Football League club in existence. Name the three older clubs.

## WORLD CUP – VI

1. How old was Roger Milla when he appeared for Cameroon in the 1994 tournament in the USA?

2. In the 1958 tournament held in Sweden, striker Just Fontaine played and scored in each of France's six games as they reached the semi-finals. But how many goals did he score in total?

3. Which one of the following were not amongst the eight seeded countries for the 2002 World Cup tournament held in South Korea and Japan – was it Croatia, Spain or South Korea?

## HE SAID WHAT? – V

### Who are responsible for these quotes?

1. "Management is a seven-day-a-week job. The intensity of it takes its toll on your health. Some people want to go on forever, and I obviously don't."

2. "Well, what a turn-up. From professional footballer, to television presenter, to Green politician. Whatever next?"

3. "Shit! Did you see that! He must have a foot like a traction engine!!!"

## SOME QUESTIONS ABOUT... IPSWICH TOWN

1. When they became Football League Champions in 1961.62, how many seasons had they spent in total in the top division?

2. In both 2003/04 and 2004/05 they reached the play-offs for promotion to the Premier League, and both times they lost to the same team. Was it Derby, Leeds or West Ham?

3. Name the three Ipswich bosses who went on to manage at international level.

## JOHN TERRY

1. Which midland club did he spend a short time on loan to in 1999/2000?

2. In 2001/02 he became a regular in the Chelsea team. Who did he form a successful defensive partnership with?

3. What was significant about his goal for England against Brazil in June 2007?

## CUP FINAL COLOURS – II

**What colours did these clubs wear
in the following FA Cup Finals?**

1. Man C (v Leicester) in 1968/69.

2. Arsenal (v Liverpool) in 1949/50.

3. Man C (v Birmingham) in 1955/56.

## SOME QUESTIONS ABOUT...
## HEART OF MIDLOTHIAN

1. On the final day of 1985/86 Hearts were ten minutes away from their first Scottish title since 1960, when Dundee scored twice, and their main rivals for the title won 5-0 to pip them on goal-difference. Who were these rivals – Dundee Utd, Celtic or Aberdeen?

2. Due to Tynecastle not meeting UEFA criteria for hosting European football, where did they play their 'home' games in the 2006/07 Champions League?

3. Dave Mackay began his career with Hearts and captained them to the title in 1957/58. He then joined Spurs and won the 'double'. But who did he manage to the Football League Championship in 1974/75?

## THE 1990s – VI

1. In 1998/99 Spurs and Newcastle finished 11th and 13th respectively in the Premier League. However, they both qualified to play in the following seasons UEFA Cup. How?

2. When Colchester won promotion back to the Football League in 1991/92, which club went the other way down to the Conference?

3. In 1993/94 the Premier League took a sponsor on board. Who were they?

## STRIKING FOR GLORY – VI

1. Which striker holds the record for the most FA Cup Final goals – is it Geoff Hurst, Alan Shearer or Ian Rush?

2. What record did Roger Milla (Camaroon) break when he scored against Russia at the World Cup in 1994?

3. In 1958/59 Jimmy Greaves, Brian Clough, Jim Towers and Arthur Rowley were the top scorers in the four English divisions. Which clubs were they playing for?

## SOME QUESTIONS ABOUT... BOSTON UNITED

1. Which future Birmingham, Portsmouth and Derby boss cut his managerial teeth with Boston in 1969?

2. Which former England midfielder played his final four league games for them in 2004/05?

3. Although Boston won the Northern Premier League in 1977/78, their ground was not deemed fit for the Division 4. However, the runners-up were put forward and elected to take Southport's place in the Football League. Who were they?

## FA CUP – VI

1. What do the cup winning teams of WBA (1888), Bolton (1958), Man C (1969) and West Ham (1975) have in common?

2. Bob Stokoe and Don Revie were rival managers for Sunderland and Leeds in the 1972/73 final. However, they also came up against each other as players in the 1955 final. Which clubs were they playing for?

3. In 1992/93 both semi-finals were played at Wembley for the first time. Why?

## PRAWN SANDWICH ANYONE? – III

**If you were sharing an executive box with these celebrity fans, which two teams might you be watching?**

1. Popular '60s crooner Engelbert Humperdinck and Slade's Noddy Holder.

2. Salman 'Satanic Verses' Rushdie and heavy metal icon Ozzy Osbourne.

3. Ray "I'm the daddy" Winstone and 'Tiger' Tim Henman.

## SOME QUESTIONS ABOUT... ASTON VILLA

1. When Villa piped Ipswich to the Football League title in 1980/81, how many players did they use throughout the season?

2. Influential in the founding of Villa were two Scotsmen named George Ramsay and William McGregor. But which two Scottish clubs allegedly inspired their choice of claret and light blue as the team colours?

3. Prior to 2008/09, who was the last English born manager of Villa?

## MURPHY'S DRAGONS

1. What other job was Jimmy Murphy holding down when he took Wales to the 1958 World Cup in Sweden?

2. Two sets of brothers were named in the 22-man squad. Name them.

3. Who scored the only goal against Wales in the quarter-final, which brought Murphy's World Cup campaign to an end?

## GETTING THERE – VI

**Arriving at the railway station, you jump in a cab. This is the route your taxi takes. But which ground are you heading to?**

It's nearly two miles. Head south on Sherwood Drive and turn left into Buckingham Rd. At the roundabout, take the first exit onto Saxon St. At the Denbigh Roundabout, take the first exit onto Bletcham Way and at the next roundabout, take the second exit onto Grafton St. Take the next right and you're there.

# SOME QUESTIONS ABOUT... GREECE

1. How many of the 22-man squad that went to the 1994 World Cup tournament were used?

2.There was only one Premier League player who appeared in Greece's victory over Portugal in the final of Euro 2004 – was it Nikos Dabizas (Leicester), Stelios Giannakopoulos (Bolton) or Vassilis Lakis (Crystal Palace)?

3. Which Ulsterman managed Greece between 1971 and 1973?

## THE 1980s – VI

1. In March 1987 which Sunderland legend was re-appointed as manager in an attempt to save the club from relegation to Division 3?

2. Which future England striker made his debut as a substitute for Southampton in a Division 1 fixture against Chelsea on March 26th 1988?

3. At the end of the 1982/83, which Milan-born manager took over Crewe Alexandra?

## AT THE MOVIES – II

### Three plots from football-based movies. Name them.

1. A series of events lead Tommy Johnston to question his violent life and his own morals. Can he continue his life as a 'headhunter'? Meanwhile there's a 'meet' lined-up with the 'bushwackers'...

2. The summer of 1954. Eleven-year-old Matthias is the lucky mascot for a team which includes some of the country's top players. Then his father returns from a Russian POW camp, casting a shadow over his family. But Matthias rekindles his love of life and also 'helps' his country win the World Cup...

3. Much to her traditionalist parents' dismay, an 18 year-old lives to play football rather than learning to cook and finding a husband...

## SOME QUESTIONS ABOUT... BRADFORD CITY

1. What was used from 1910/11 to 1990/91, and what place does Bradford have in it's history?

2. Which World Cup winner ended his career at City, where he also acted briefly as caretaker-manager?

3. Following the tragic fire in May 1985 City used Elland Rd (Leeds) and Leeds Rd (Huddersfield) before settling into their temporary 'home'. Was it Odsal Stadium, Park Avenue or The Shay?

## HOME OF THE BRAVE – VI

1. If you were at Ochilview Park and 'The Warriors' were playing 'The Staggies', which game would you be watching?

2. Why, in 1994/95, might they have been "Dancing in the streets of Kirkcaldy"?

3. Tommy Coyne was three times top scorer in the Scottish Premier League with three different clubs. Who were they?

## SEQUENCES – VI

### Who is next in the following sequences?

1. Ally MacLeod, Jock Stein, Alex Ferguson, ___?___.

2. David Coleman, Jimmy Hill, Des Lynam, ___?___.

3. Carlisle, Hereford, Morecambe, ___?___.

# SOME QUESTIONS ABOUT... CRYSTAL PALACE

1. Name two Palace players who went on to not only manage the team, but also England.

2. In the 1989/90 FA Cup Final, Ian Wright famously came off the bench to score two goals and force a replay. But who scored their opening goal – was it Mark Bright, Alan Pardew or Gary O'Reilly?

3. In November 1961 Johnny Byrne, Palace's 22 year-old striker, became one of only five players to date to do what?

## EUROPEAN SILVERWARE – VI

1. When Ryan Giggs replaced Paul Scholes in the 87th minute of the 2008 Champions League Final, he passed Bobby Charlton's record of first team appearances for Man Utd. But how many games had Charlton played – was it 687, 758 or 902?

2. What was the official attendance at Wembley when AC Milan beat Benfica in the 1963 European Cup Final – was it 45,000, 78,000 or 100,000?

3. Only three clubs have won all three of Europe's major trophies – The European Cup/Champions League, The European Cup-Winners Cup and the Fairs/UEFA Cup. Name them.

## ANOTHER BITE AT THE CHERRY? – IV

Which seven members of Celtic's 1967 European Cup winning 'Lisbon Lions' went to Milan three years later only to lose to Feyenoord in the final of the same competition?

## SOME QUESTIONS ABOUT... USA

1. In 1992 Mike Masters earned a single cap for the USA as a substitute in a 0-0 against Uruguay. A month earlier he had become the first American to score at Wembley when his opening goal enabled his club to attain the non-league 'double' and return to the Football League. Who were they?

2. In the USA's famous 1950 World Cup victory over England, Joe Gaetjens scored the decisive goal. Which country was he actually born in – was it Haiti, Scotland or Belgium?

3. Cobi Jones played 164 times for the USA. But which English club did he play for between 1992 and 1995?

## THE 1970s – VI

1. Name the manager who was sacked in December 1970 having fallen into the shadow of his legendary predecessor?

2. In 1975/76, which club became the first former Football League Champions to play in Division 4?

3. In November 1972 two former Scunthorpe players made their debuts for England in a World Cup qualifier against Wales. Name them.

## BY MUTUAL CONSENT? – VI

### Identify the well-known manager from the following clues.

His first club had a cutting-edge and he went onto play for military ammunition, shay men and little devils, before combining roles with eastern pilgrims and oystermen where he gained his first promotion. He moved to Lancastrian rovers and second city blues before leading academics to consecutive promotions. After a fall-out with a dodgy media proprietor, he moved to bush men who were ironically beaten by his previous club at Wembley the following year. There were then spells with members of the crow family, southern sailors and horned sheep. He assisted with sky blues and then twice with an old hammer down south before returning to help a city of spires that had fallen under dubious ownership again.

## SOME QUESTIONS ABOUT... HARTLEPOOL UNITED

1. Which player who began and ended his career with Hartlepool, scored an FA Cup Final goal which was voted Match of the Day's 'Goal of the Season'?

2. Who began his managerial career at Hartlepool in October 1965?

3. In 1986/87 which club were locked out of their own ground by the bailiffs, and staged their opening 'home' game of the season at Hartlepool?

## THE WORLD GAME – VI

1. In 1998 Fan Zhiyi and Sun Jihai became the first Chinese players to sign for an English club. Who did they join?

2. Claude Makelele and José Bosingwa are full internationals with France and Portugal respectively. But in which country were they both born?

3. What was significant about the match between Austria and Hungary played in Vienna in 1902?

# HOW MUCH? – VI

1. In 1994 who became the most expensive player to be transferred between English clubs, and who did he form a strike-partnership with known as 'SAS'?

2. In 1999 who joined Coventry from Wolves for £6m, and in doing so became the most expensive British teenager?

3. Who left an English port for a German port for £0.5m in 1977?

# SOME QUESTIONS ABOUT...
## WOLVERHAMPTON WANDERERS

1. To date, Wolves have employed six bosses who have managed at international level – two for Scotland, two for England, and one each for Saudi Arabia and the Republic of Ireland. Name them.

2. Peter Knowles was one of the brightest stars of the late '60s. But his life took a dramatic turn in 1970 when he left football to become a Jehovah's Witness. In what year did Wolves finally terminate his registration – was it 1977, 1982 or 1990?

3. In 1954 what was the indirect consequence of Wolves beating Honvad of Hungary in a floodlit exhibition game at Molineux, and declaring themselves unofficial champion club of the world'?

# STEVE COPPELL

1. With which club did he start his playing career?

2. How old was he when he retired due to a knee injury – 23, 28 or 31?

3. In 1996 which club did he manage for just 33 days?

## SIGN ON THE DOTTED LINE, SON – VI

**Name the clubs that the following players
first signed with as professionals.**

1. Alex Stepney.

2. Kevin Davies.

3. Perry Groves.

## SOME QUESTIONS ABOUT...
## TRANMERE ROVERS

1. Who led them to two FA Cup quarter-finals in 1999/2000 and 2000/01, and a League Cup Final in 1999/2000?

2. On Boxing Day 1935, 'Bunny' Bell scored nine goals and missed a penalty in a record-breaking Division 3 (North) fixture against Oldham. What was the final score – was it 10-7, 16-1 or 13-4?

3. Which former Liverpool stopper managed Rovers from 1972 to 1975, bringing in ex-teammate Ian St John and using Bill Shankly as a consultant?

## THE 1960s – VI

1. On October 30th 1960, in a shantytown on the southern outskirts of Buenos Aires, a future world star was born. Who was he?

2. What 'double' did QPR achieve in 1966/67?

3. Where were these future England managers playing or managing at the end of the 1964/65 season – Ron Greenwood, Terry Venables, Bobby Robson and caretakers Joe Mercer and Howard Wilkinson?

## THAT'S MY BOY! – II

### What were the first league management jobs
### for these father and sons?

1. John and Paul Trollope.

2. John and Kevin Bond.

3. Don and Gary Megson.


## SOME QUESTIONS ABOUT... LEICESTER CITY

1. How many FA Cup finals have Leicester played in and, of those, how many have they won?

2. In 1995 Mark McGhee unexpectedly left to take charge at Wolves. Who took over and led Leicester to their most successful spell in modern times?

3. In 2007 who took over in May and left 'by mutual consent' in August?


## THREE LIONS – VI

1. Ian Callaghan won what appeared to be his second and last England cap against France during the 1966 World Cup. But how long was it before he received a surprise call-up for a friendly international against Switzerland – was it 6 years & 8 months, 11 years & 2 months or 14 years & 3 months?

2. Who was full-time manager of England between 1946 and 1963?

3. Although England first played at Wembley in 1924, it wasn't until 1951 that another nation, apart from Scotland, was invited to play there. Who were they?

## STAT-TASTIC – VI

### Identify the player from the following career statistics.

Born: Woolwich, London.
League Career Span: 1985/86 to 1999/2000.
International Caps: 31 apps – 9 goals.

| CLUB/NICKNAME | LEAGUE APPS | GOALS |
|---|---|---|
| Eagles | 225 | 89 |
| Gunners | 221 | 128 |
| Hammers | 22 | 9 |
| Forest (loan) | 10 | 5 |
| Bhoys | 8 | 3 |
| Clarets | 15 | 4 |

## SOME QUESTIONS ABOUT... NOTTS COUNTY

1. Have they, to date, played in the Premier League?

2. Which County 15 year old joined Arsenal for £2m in 1999?

3. Despite Meadow Lane lying just 300 metres away from Nott'm Forest's City Ground, what 'obstacle' also separates them?

## JIMMY JOHNSTONE

1. How did England full-back Terry Cooper describe him after the European Cup semi-final encounter between Leeds and Celtic in 1970?
a) "A bit tricky."
b) "More slippery than a bag of eels."
c) "My nightmare."

2. What was his nickname?

3. Which was the only English clubs he played for?

## INTO THE LEAGUE! – III

### Guess the club from the details of their first ever home league game.

OPPOSITION: Derby.
LEAGUE: Football League.
DATE: September 8th 1888.
HOME GROUND: Pike's Lane.
COLOURS: White shirts, navy blue knickers and stockings.

## SOME QUESTIONS ABOUT...ITALY

1. The semi-final of the 1970 Mexico World Cup became known as 'The Game of the Century'. With the scores level after 90 minutes, five goals were scored in extra time. Italy won 4-3 but who were their opponents that day?

2. In March 1949 Italy convincingly beat Spain 3-1 in Madrid. Less than six weeks later, six of the Italian players who played that day would be killed in the Superga plane crash. Their club had been Serie 'A' Champions for the previous three seasons. Which club was it?

3. Born in Ashton-under-Lyne, Roma midfielder Simone Perrotta was the last English-born player to collect a World Cup winners medal when he represented Italy in the 2006 final. If he were to join the league club nearest to his birthplace, which club would it be – Stockport, Oldham or Man C?

## PRE-1960s – VI

1. Which multi-title winning manager made his debut as a player for Liverpool in an FA Cup 3rd Round, 1st leg game at Chester on January 5th 1946?

2. The oldest club in Italy have been champions nine times, and four-times runners-up. But have not reached these heights since 1929/30. Name them.

3. Which clubs won the European Cup during the 1950s?

## EURO '96 AND ALL THAT – III

1. Alan Shearer top-scored with five goals for the tournament. Four players were equal-second with three goals apiece. One was German, one Bulgarian, one Croatian and one Danish. Name them.

2. Name the eight stadiums used during the tournament.

3. Who scored Scotland's only goal of the tournament in their 1-0 win over Switzerland?

## SOME QUESTIONS ABOUT...
## COLCHESTER UNITED

1. In 1948/49 Layer Road had its record attendance of 19,072 for an FA Cup tie against Reading. However, the game was abandoned. Was it because of crowd trouble, fog or a broken goalpost?

2. The 1991/92 Conference season was a two-horse-race between Colchester and Wycombe. When they met at Adams Park, the U's won 2-1 with an injury time winner. But what was unusual about the goal?

3. Which current athletics broadcaster and former Olympic gold medallist had an uncle who captained the U's to a remarkable FA Cup 5th Round victory over Don Revie's Leeds in 1970/71?

## EURO CHAMPIONSHIPS – VI

1. Which Scandinavian country made their tournament debut in Euro 2000?

2. Name the three Spurs players chosen for the 22-man England squad that travelled to Italy for Euro '68?

3. Which stadium hosted it's second Euro Championship Final in 1980 – was it Stadio Comunale (Turin), Stadio San Paolo (Naples) or Stadio Olimpico (Rome)?

## OLD GROUNDS FOR NEW – III

**Which clubs used to play their home
games at the following grounds?**

1. Sealand Road.

2. Somerton Park.

3. Burnden Park.

## SOME QUESTIONS ABOUT... INTER MILAN

1. When Inter won their first European Cup in 1964, only three other clubs had previously won the trophy since its inception in 1956. Name them.

2. Which Croydon born boss had two spells as Inter's manager in the 1990s?

3. How many seasons have Inter spent outside Serie 'A'?

## TODAY'S THE DAY – VI

**Identify the major news story that occurred on the day when
the following events were happening in the world of football**

It is announced that the FA will receive £11,500 per game from the BBC or ITV for coverage of future internationals at Wembley. Bury record their sixth game without victory as they lose to a Dave Galvin goal at home to Gillingham. After a thigh injury, Liverpool striker John Toshack declares himself fit for tomorrows trip to Newcastle, and Norman Hunter, Terry Cooper and Mick Jones plan to make their comebacks after injury for Leeds Reserves at Aston Villa.
Meanwhile at Conservative Central Office...

# ME! ME! ME! – VII

### From the following description, guess who I am.

I was born in London, raised an Essex boy and carefully nurtured by north-western reds. I scored my first league goal whilst briefly on loan to lilywhites. On returning 'home' I became the central focus in a team of prodigiously talented youngsters and experienced campaigners who would, in the following seasons, sweep all before them. Sublime skills, glorious goals, doubtful discipline and a spicy union have guaranteed that I receive worship and vilification in equal measures. The red-tops have cooled a bit, but I used to be a top tabloid-shifting commodity. I became a £25m 'Galacticos' and copped over 100 caps – even though I now play 'sexy' football near movie-land. For a time I was probably the most famous man on the planet.

## SOME QUESTIONS ABOUT... FULHAM

1. Which player whose Fulham career spanned 18 years, was known as 'Mr. Fulham' or 'The Maestro'?

2. In 1997 having sacked Micky Adams, Mohamed Al-Fayed installed his 'dream team'. Who were they?

3. What do Johnny Haynes, Karl-Heinz Riedle and Ray Lewington have in common?

## THE 2000s – VII

1. In September 2006 American entrepreneur Randy Lerner officially became chairman of Aston Villa. Which legendary figure did he replace?

2. What did the only two league clubs in Essex achieve at the end of the 2005/06?

3. Fulham, Bolton and Blackburn were promoted to the Premier League in 2000/01. But which of them survived the following season to remain in the top tier?

# CLIMBING UP THE PYRAMID

1. the Conference was created in 1979/80. Only two of its former members have so far made it to the Championship (tier 2). Name them.

2. Which Lancashire club folded after having had a meteoric rise through the pyramid system between 1982 and 1989, when they were refused entry into the Conference because their ground was not to standard?

3. Which club won the first two seasons of the Conference but still have not, as yet, played in the Football League – is it Altrincham, Runcorn or Enfield?

# SOME QUESTIONS ABOUT... SOUTHPORT

1. The scorers of all Blackpool's goals in their famous 4-3 FA Cup Final victory over Bolton in 1953 ended their Football League playing careers with Southport. Name them.

2. Who left the 'hot-seat' at Southport to take over as manager of N. Ireland in 1967 – was it Terry Neill, Billy Bingham or Danny Blanchflower?

3. In 1918 Southport took the name Southport Vulcan for just one season. What was 'Vulcan' and why was this a pioneering move by the club?

# WORLD CUP – VII

1. Name the 15 Arsenal players who were on duty for their respective countries in the 2006 World Cup final tournament?

2. Uruguay and Brazil played the final game of the 1950 tournament in Rio's Maracanā Stadium. What was the official attendance – was it 98,000, 112,873 or 199,954?

3. What is generally believed to have been the fate of the Jules Rimet trophy following its theft in 1983?

## SKIPPER! – II

**Name the cup final, the year and the clubs involved
when the following captains led out their teams.**

1. Matt Elliot and Dave Challinor.

2. Theodoros Zagorakis and Luis Figo.

3. Lothar Matthäus and Bixente Lizarazu.

## SOME QUESTIONS ABOUT... LIVERPOOL

1. As of 2008 Real Madrid have contested twelve European Cup finals, and AC Milan eleven. Along with three other clubs Liverpool have contested seven. Name those other clubs.

2. How many European trophies' did Liverpool win during the reign of Bill Shankly?

3. From the 1960s through to the 1980s the manager and coaching staff would informally meet to drink tea, discuss the team and tactics, and work out how they were going to beat their next opponents. This meeting place became legendary. What was it called, and what was its primary purpose?

## GERD MÜLLER

1. He gained 62 caps for W. Germany. But how many goals did he score – was it 51, 68 or 79?

2. Which two other future internationals and World Cup winners were playing for the then second tier Bayern Munich when Müller signed in 1964?

3. What was his nickname?

## WHO'S MISSING? – IV

**Below are eight of the starting line-up when
England lost to Germany in the semi-final of Euro '96.
Name the three missing players.**

David Seaman, Gareth Southgate, Stuart Pearce, \_\_\_?\_\_\_, Paul Ince, \_\_\_?\_\_\_, Darren Anderton, Paul Gascoigne, Alan Shearer, Teddy Sheringham, \_\_\_?\_\_\_.

## SOME QUESTIONS ABOUT... BRENTFORD

1. In the early '60s which future rock/pop star was an apprentice with The Bees – was it Keith Richards, Syd Barrett or Rod Stewart?

2. In 1929/30 Brentford won promotion from Division 3 (South). But how many points did they drop at 'home' that season?

3. In January 1967 which club proposed a take-over of Brentford?

## THE 1990s – VII

1. When former Italian international Attilio Lombardo took over at a struggling Crystal Palace towards the end of 1997/98, he spoke little English. Which Swede assisted him and interpreted his instructions for the players?

2. In 1991/92, which chairman told Newcastle manager Ossie Ardiles that his job was safe just 36 hours before sacking him?

3. On August 19th 1993, the man who steered Aston Villa to European Cup glory in 1982 died of a heart attack aged 56. Who was he?

## STRIKING FOR GLORY – VII

1. What were the consequences of Andrés Escobar's own-goal in the World Cup 1994 game between Colombia and USA?

2. In 1971/72, Francis Lee (Man C) became Division 1 top scorer with 33 goals. How many were penalties – was it 13, 19 or none at all?

3. Robert Prosinecki scored for two different countries in two separate World Cups. Name the countries.

## SOME QUESTIONS ABOUT... WALSALL

1. Which player who started his career at Walsall, scored on his debut for England in a World Cup tournament?

2. In a 3rd Round FA Cup tie in 1933, Walsall of Division 3 (North) beat a team who were on the verge of winning the Football League title for the first of three consecutive times. Who were they and who was their legendary manager?

3. Walsall 'keeper Clayton Ince is currently the most capped goalkeeper for which country?

## FA CUP – VII

1. In 1991 Nott'm Forest's Mark Crossley became only the second goalkeeper to save a penalty in an FA Cup Final at Wembley. Whose penalty did he save?

2. In 1889 Preston won the League title without being beaten, and the FA Cup without conceding a goal. As a result what did they become known as – was it 'The Incredibles', 'The Unbeatables' or 'The Invincibles'?

3. Only four men to date have both played for and managed the same cup winning team. Name them.

## LATIN HOMEWORK – II

**Three traditional nicknames and mottos.
Name the club and translate the motto.**

1. Black Cats – Consectatio Excellentiae.

2. Shakers – Vincit Omnia Industria.

3. Rovers – Ubi Fides ibi Lux et Robur.


## SOME QUESTIONS ABOUT... PORT VALE

1. Which of the following never played for Vale; Stanley Matthews, Mark Bright, Marcus Bent or Robbie Earle?

2. In the 1953/54 FA Cup 6th Round, they were drawn away to Leyton Orient. Vale were in Division 3 (North) at the time, but what division were their opponents in?

3. When, in the late 1940s, ambitious plans were put in place to build Vale Park with a 70,000 capacity, what was the projected stadium christened?


## THREE LIONS ALTERNATIVE STRIP

**England's second colours have traditionally been
red shirts, white shorts and red socks. But what kit
did they wear for the following games?**

1. v Czechoslovakia (1970 World Cup Group 3 – Mexico).

2. v Poland (1974 World Cup qualifier – Chorzow).

3. v Germany (Euro '96 semi-finals – Wembley).

## GETTING THERE – VII

**Arriving at the railway station, you jump in a cab. This is the route your taxi takes. But which ground are you heading to?**

It's about two and a half miles. Head south on North Bridge. Turn right at Market St and at the roundabout take the 1st exit onto the A8. Turn left at Princes St and continue on the A8 before turning left at Torphichen St and follow the road round into Morrison St. Take a slight left at Dalry Rd, turn right at Murieston Crescent and follow the road into McLeod St. Follow McLeod St and the stadium is on your right.

## SOME QUESTIONS ABOUT...
## SHEFFIELD UNITED

1. Which future England caretaker began his managerial career with The Blades in 1955?

2. Which of the following has Bramall Lane not hosted: A senior England football international, a cricket Test match, an FA Cup Final or an audience with Pope John Paul II?

3. What do Sheff Utd and the World Snooker Championship have in common?

## THE 1980s – VII

1. On February 27th 1987 details were announced regarding a proposed merger between which two South London clubs. Who were they?

2. Which 17 year-old Ulsterman made his debut for Man Utd on April 24th 1982 away at Brighton?

3. In October 1988, which future TV pundit was sacked as manager of Oxford following a dispute with the club's directors over the sale of striker Dean Saunders to Derby?

## ... WAIT A MINUTE MR POSTMAN – III

### Identify the stadium and the clubs that play at these postal locations.

1. B_____ R___, Seasiders Way, FY1 6JJ

2. F____ M___, Quarry Lane NG18 5DA

3. B_____ P___, Furtherwood Rd, OL1 2PA

## SOME QUESTIONS ABOUT... QUEEN OF THE SOUTH

1. In which southern Scottish town are Queen of the South based?

2. Some scenes for the 1999 film 'A Shot At Glory' were shot at their home ground at Palmerston Park. Ally McCoist was a co-star, but which two American actors appeared alongside him in the roles of the club coach and club owner?

3. Which Newcastle and Chelsea legend started his career with Queen of the South in 1920 – was it Jackie Milburn, Hughie Gallacher or Alex James?

## HOME OF THE BRAVE – VII

1. In 2004/05 who finished eighth in their first season of top-flight football?

2. The names Brookes Mileson, Rowan Alexander and 'Dr' Kenny Deucher are associated with which former Scottish League club?

3. Jock Wallace, who would go on to manage Rangers, Leicester and Sevilla, was player-manager of Berwick when they shocked the football world by beating Rangers in the Scottish FA Cup. What position did he play?

## SEQUENCES – VII

### Who is next in the following sequences?

1. Ron Greenwood, Bobby Robson, Glenn Hoddle, ___?___.

2. West Ham, Watford, Derby Co, ___?___.

3. Old Trafford, Emirates Stadium, St James' Park, ___?___.

## SOME QUESTIONS ABOUT... DERBY COUNTY

1. Who, in the 1980s, was 'Fat, and round, and never at the ground'?

2. Name two Derby managers who have gone on to manage Scotland.

3. In July 2007, a trophy was introduced to be awarded to the winners of future meetings between Derby and rivals Nott'm Forest. What is it called – The East Midlands Cup, The Brian Clough Trophy or The McGovern Cup?

.

## EUROPEAN SILVERWARE – VII

1. To date three English teams and three Scottish teams have reached their only UEFA Cup Final and lost. Name them.

2. In May 2008 Ronaldo, Carlos Tevez, Wayne Rooney and Nemanja Vidic came home from Moscow with Champions League winners medals. But which clubs were they with as youth team players when Man Utd last won the trophy in 1998/99?

3. Who coached Lazio to UEFA Cup success in 1998/99?

## BENCHWARMING – III

The following substitutions were made in League Cup finals. Name the year and the clubs that were playing each other.

1. Lou Macari replaced Kevin Moran and David Fairclough replaced Craig Johnston.

2. Ian Bowyer replaced Mike Summerbee and Dick Krzywicki replaced Asa Hartford.

3. Rod Belfitt replaced Eddie Gray and Terry Neill replaced David Jenkins.

## SOME QUESTIONS ABOUT... GATESHEAD

1. In an echo of MK Dons takeover of Wimbledon, 1930/31 kicked off with Gateshead as a brand new Division 3 (North) club. They had taken over the Football League status of another club and had moved it lock, stock and barrel from a town that was over ten miles away. Who was this club?

2. In 1951/52 they played WBA in a home FA Cup 4th Round tie. But in order to accommodate nearly 40,000 spectators, where was the game played?

3. In 1959/60 which club were elected to replace Gateshead?

## THE 1970s – VII

1. In October 1975 which bespectacled comedian and scriptwriter, best known for his silent comedy film classic 'The Plank', was offered and accepted an invitation to join the board of his hometown club, Oldham?

2. Name the clubs or country's that former Leeds players – Billy Bremner, Jack Charlton, Allan Clarke, Johnny Giles and Don Revie – were managing at the close of the 1970s?

3. After his team finished bottom of the Football League in 1971/72, manager Ernie Tagg allegedly took the unusual step of sacking himself. Which club was it?

# BY MUTUAL CONSENT? – VII

### Identify the well-known manager from the following clues.

From a Scottish underground heritage emerged a man who would become one of the few genuine legends of the game. His career embraced Cumbrians and north enders where he both lost and won a domestic cup in consecutive seasons. A promising career, which included caps at international level, was interrupted by the war. His first management role was an undistinguished stint with his first club. Spells with seafarers, north-western reds and Yorkshire terriers eventually led to one of footballs greatest appointments. Arriving to find his red charges at the bottom of the second tier, he laid the foundations for what would become one of the most successful club sides in the world. He shocked football by retiring at his peak, but, to a great degree, his work was done.

# SOME QUESTIONS ABOUT... HOLLAND

1. The term 'Total Football' is usually associated with which coach and which player?

2. Which two countries did they lose to in the 1974 and the 1978 World Cup Final?

3. Which goalkeeper is currently Holland's most capped player – is it Piet Schrijvers, Edwin van der Sar or Hans van Breukelen?

# THE WORLD GAME – VII

1. Which club did 1970 World Cup winners Carlos Alberto, Clodoaldo and Pelé play for?

2. During the Soviet era, Spartak Moscow were owned by the Collective Production Farms. What was their nickname – was it 'The Butchers', 'The Turnips' or 'The Meat'?

3. Which club won their first French title in 2001/02 and subsequently retained it for the next six seasons?

## WHAT'S IN A NICKNAME? – III

### Guess the club or clubs from this description of their nickname.

These are people who travel long distances to places of religious or historic significance. In this instance they were 17th century European settlers in New England.

## SOME QUESTIONS ABOUT...
## CREWE ALEXANDRA

1. What are the origins of the name 'Alexandra'?
a) Princess Alexandra visited the town in 1876.
b) '54 Alexandra' – an asteroid that allegedly landed nearby in 1858.
c) Named after the pub next door to the ground.

2. Which one of the following did not make his first Football League appearance as a Crewe player: Danny Murphy, Dean Ashton, Bruce Grobbelaar, Neil Lennon, Robbie Savage or David Platt?

3. In 1959/60 Crewe held one of Division 1's top sides to a 2-2 draw at Gresty Rd in the FA Cup 4th Round. However, they lost the replay 13-2. This was a record defeat and victory for both teams respectively. Who were their opponents?

## LUIS FIGO

1. Which Dutchman signed Figo for Barcelona in 1995?

2. In 2002 he returned to the Nou Camp with Real Madrid. What unusual object did angry Barcelona fans throw at him during the match?

3. With which Portuguese club did he begin his career?

# SIGN ON THE DOTTED LINE, SON – VII

### Name the clubs that the following players first signed with as professionals.

1. Paul Dickov.

2. Tom Huddlestone.

3. Emlyn Hughes.


## SOME QUESTIONS ABOUT... WREXHAM

1. In 1975/76 Wrexham narrowly lost on aggregate in the European Cup-Winners' Cup quarter-final. Their Belgian conquerors would go on to beat West Ham in the final. Who were they?

2. Which Welsh legend wound-up his league career when he signed for Wrexham in the summer of 1998, but failed to score in 18 appearances?

3. Wrexham's Racecourse Ground is officially the oldest football stadium in the world still hosting internationals. But who did Wales play in their first 'home' game in 1877?


## THE 1960s – VII

1. Who, in 1966, was dubbed 'El Quinto Beatle' by the Portuguese press following an impressive display against Benfica in a European Cup quarter-final?

2. In 1968/69 Leeds, Derby, Watford and Doncaster won their respective divisional titles in the Football League. Name their managers and what the four of them had in common?

3. In 1967/68 who had managed Oxford on a journey from the Southern League to the Football League Division 2 in just six seasons – was it Stan Cullis, Ron Atkinson or Arthur Turner?

## TAKING THE MIC – II

**You've seen or heard him on the telly. Guess who it is.**

This son of Kent and devotee of his local team began radio broadcasting with the BBC in 1961 and remained with them until 1967. He covered all the major domestic and European finals during that period including England's World Cup triumph in 1966 when he was the main commentator for BBC Radio. Having been enticed to ITV by Jimmy Hill, he became their football anchorman for the next thirty-or-so years. In 1970 he chaired ITV's World Cup coverage. This included, for the first time, a lively studio panel of experts, which caused viewers to desert the more staid BBC coverage in droves. He retired as a commentator after the 1998 World Cup Final. This most popular of men died on the same day that England beat Germany 5-1 in Munich.

## SOME QUESTIONS ABOUT...
## MELCHESTER ROVERS

1. In which year did 'Roy of the Rovers' first appear in 'Tiger' comic – was it 1945, 1954 or 1966?

2. Why did Melchester spend most of the 1988/89 season using Wembley Stadium as their 'home' ground?

3. What are the predominant colours of Melchester?

## THREE LIONS – VII

1. Which two former England managers were born in Yorkshire?

2. How long was it between Stanley Matthews making his England debut, and his 54th and final cap – was it 15 years & 11 months, 22 years & 8 months or 28 years & 3 months?

3. Which of the following players have  never worn the captain's armband following the substitution of the official England captain – Jamie Carragher, Robbie Fowler, Emile Heskey, Jamie Redknapp, Phil Neville or Gareth Barry?

## STAT-TASTIC – VII

**Identify the player from the following career statistics.**

Born: Plymouth.
League Career Span: 1970/71 to 1993/94.
International Caps: 52 apps – 12 goals.

| CLUB/NICKNAME | LEAGUE APPS | GOALS |
|---|---|---|
| Blues | 280 | 119 |
| The Express (loan) | 33 | 36 |
| Forest | 70 | 28 |
| Citizens | 26 | 12 |
| Blucerchiati | 68 | 17 |
| Orobici | 21 | 1 |
| Gers | 18 | 0 |
| R's | 32 | 12 |
| Owls | 89 | 9 |

# SOME QUESTIONS ABOUT... MANSFIELD TOWN

1. In the 1968/69 FA Cup 5th Round, Mansfield humbled a high-flying West Ham 3-0. Name the four England internationals, whether established or yet to play, who appeared for the Hammers that day?

2. In 1976/77 Mansfield gained promotion to Division 2. But how many seasons in total have they spent, to date, in the 2nd tier?

3. Which former Watford, AC Milan and England striker wound-up his career with Mansfield in 1993/94?

# JEFF ASTLE

1. In the 1970 World Cup finals, Astle appeared in two group games. One was against Czechoslovakia. Who were the other opponents?

2. In 1974 Astle signed for Southern League Dunstable. Who was the manager who signed him and which legendary player did he briefly play alongside whilst he was there?

3. When Astle scored against Man C in the 1970 League Cup Final, he became the first player to achieve what?

## HOW MUCH? – VII

1. Which Dutchman signed for Chelsea on a 'Bosman' in 2000/01, and retired four years later having played just 11 games for the club while earning a basic £40,000 per week?

2. One went from Wolves to Man C – the other from Aston Villa to Wolves. Name the two £1.4m-plus players involved in these record-breaking transfers in September 1979?

3. Prior to Zinedine Zidane's £46m move from Juventus to Real Madrid, who was the last Frenchman to hold the record as 'The World's Most Expensive Player' when he went from Marseille to AC Milan for £10m in 1992 – was it Michel Platini, Alain Giresse or Jean-Pierre Papin?

## SOME QUESTIONS ABOUT... PRESTON NORTH END

1. Which three European Cup winners have managed the club?

2. Name Preston's most capped player?

3. When Preston became the first club to achieve the 'double' in 1888/89, who did they beat in the FA Cup Final – was it Wolves, Chelsea or Royal Arsenal?

## PRE-1960s – VII

1. On September 12th 1885 Dundee Harp beat Aberdeen Rovers 35-0 in a Scottish Cup 1st Round game. On the same day Arbroath played Bon Accord in the same competition. What was the score there?

2. Which Saintly member of England's World Cup winning squad made his league debut in a Division 3 (South) game against Brentford on March 16th 1957?

3. Since its formation in 1934, only two clubs have wrestled the Portuguese title away from the 'Big Three' of Benfica, Sporting Lisbon or Porto. One was Boavista in 2000/01. Who was the other in 1945/46 – was it Belenenses, Vitoria Setubal or Benfica Reserves?

## 1966 AND ALL THAT – IV

1. Which continent withdrew its nations from the qualifying rounds in protest at the lack of places allocated for the final tournament?

2. England had a squad of 22 for the tournament. Name the eleven, with their clubs, who didn't play in the World Cup Final itself.

3. In the quarter-final game between N. Korea and Portugal, what was the score after 25 minutes, and what was the final score?

## SOME QUESTIONS ABOUT... YEOVIL TOWN

1. The man who managed Fulham to the 1974/75 FA Cup Final scored as player-manager of Yeovil when, as a non-league team, they beat Division 1 side Sunderland in the FA Cup 4th Round. Name him.

2. Gary Johnson managed Yeovil into the Football League in 2002/03. But who was he national manager for prior to coming to Huish Park – was it Moldova, Latvia or Liechtenstein?

3. Which England captain briefly played as a non-contract player for the club in 1984/85?

## EURO CHAMPIONSHIPS – VII

1. Which German goal-machine scored four times in the two games he played during Euro '72?

2. Who were the three goalkeepers England took to Euro 2004 in Portugal?

3. How many sending-offs were there during the fifteen matches of Euro '88, was it one, six or none at all?

## NET MINDERS – II

In the first Premier League games of the new millennium on January 3rd 2000, these were the 16 goalkeepers on duty. Name the clubs they represented.

Andy Marriott, Paul Gerrard, Shaka Hislop, Steve Harper, David James, Mart Poom, Ian Walker, David Seaman, Tim Flowers, Pavel Srnicek, Sander Westerveld, Alec Chamberlain, Matthew Clarke, Nigel Martyn, Paul Jones and Neil Sullivan.

## SOME QUESTIONS ABOUT...
## BRIGHTON & HOVE ALBION

1. For two seasons from 1997/98, they were forced to ground share 75 miles away from their former Goldstone Ground home. Who were their landlords?

2. Gordon Smith scored one and, more famously, missed one in the 1982/83 FA Cup Final against Man Utd. But which future UEFA Cup-winner and England international scored Albion's other goal?

3. In July 1991 two fledgling managers took over a London club on a joint basis. One would go on to save Albion from relegation out of the Football League. Name both bosses and the club they managed together.

## TODAY'S THE DAY – VII

Identify the major news story that occurred on the day when the following events were happening in the world of football.

In the League Cup semi-final 1st leg, goals from Pearce and Clough give Nott'm Forest a 2-1 advantage over Coventry. Aston Villa find themselves a point behind Liverpool with two games in hand following Platt's decisive penalty against Sheff Wed. In Scotland, Graeme Souness's Rangers are seven points clear, with Celtic nowhere in sight, and in Italy AC Milan go joint top with a 3-0 victory over Napoli with goals from Massaro, Maldini and van Bastin. Meanwhile at the Victor Verster Prison outside Cape Town...

## ME! ME! ME! – VIII

### From the following description, guess who I am.

I started with a local Ulster team before travelling across the water to join flying stingers. After a year I moved down the lane where I spent over a dozen years, winning domestic cups and personal plaudits. I even had the rare distinction of scoring in a charity game against red devils. When they thought I was past it, I joined their fiercest local rivals where I spent another eight years and played in three successive FA Cup finals – though winning only one. On the world scene, a maverick genius and myself made our debuts together against dragons, and I went on to win a record 119 caps. I finished my international career on my 41st birthday.

## SOME QUESTIONS ABOUT... PARTICK THISTLE

1. In 1971/72 Partick famously demolished Celtic 4-1 in the League Cup Final. The older brother of a future Thistle, Liverpool and Scotland star was playing right-back for them on that day. Who was it?

2. Which goalkeeper is their most capped player with 51 Scottish caps whilst playing for The Jags – is it Ronnie Simpson, Jim Leighton or Alan Rough?

3. Which striker was sold to Watford in 1992, and went on to be an FA Cup Final runner-up in 1993/94?

## THE 2000s – VIII

1. On August 13th 2000 the last game involving Premier League clubs was played at Wembley prior to its re-build. Who were the teams and what was the occasion?

2. Name the two former Football League Champions who began 2008/09 in League One (3rd tier)?

3. On May 24th 2008 Hull achieved two 'firsts'. What were they?

## MR CHAIRMAN – II

### Name these well known chairmen.

1. Grew up supporting QPR. Made his fortune in haulage, quarrying, ready-mix concrete and dairy farming. Was chairman of lancastrian athletes for a time in the 1960s...

2. One of the best-loved comedians between the 1930s and the 1960s. Fast-talking and quick-witted, his catch phrase was "You lucky people!"...

3. Made his fortune in meat packaging. Died of a heart attack following a TV investigation into his alleged involvement in bribing school officials for lucrative contracts, and also supplying condemned meat to schools...

## SOME QUESTIONS ABOUT... CHARLTON ATHLETIC

1. Which two clubs did they ground-share with between 1985 and 1992?

2. Former 'European Footballer of the Year' Allan Simonsen joined Charlton in a shock move from Barcelona in 1983. But which player effectively took his place at the Nou Camp?

3. Which former manager's brother managed The Who and Marc Bolan?

## WORLD CUP – VIII

1. Which two countries contested the infamous 'Battle Of Berne' during the 1954 World Cup tournament?

2. What means of deciding a drawn game was introduced for the 1998 World Cup, and which country became the first in its history to benefit?

3. When Italy retained the World Cup in 1938, where did Vice-President of FIFA, Dr Ottorino Barassi hide the Jules Rimet trophy to ensure that it didn't fall into enemy hands during World War II – was it in a shoebox under his bed, in a tin box buried in his garden or inside the cistern of his toilet?

# HE SAID WHAT? – VI

## Who are responsible for these quotes?

1. "I have played the Barcelona v Real Madrid match, but it's nothing like Boca v River. I feel like my chest burns. It's like sleeping with Julia Roberts."

2. "I spent a lot of money on booze, birds and fast cars. The rest I just squandered."

3. "The only thing I have in common with George Best is that we come from the same place, play for the same club and were discovered by the same man."

# SOME QUESTIONS ABOUT... OLDHAM ATHLETIC

1. Who beat the Latics in the FA Cup semi-finals of both 1989/90 and 1993/94?

2. Gunnar Halle is their most capped player winning 24 of his 64 caps whilst playing for the Latics. Which country did he represent?

3. Boundary Park, at 509 feet, is the third highest ground above sea-level in the top four English divisions. Which two clubs are higher?

# CHARLIE NICHOLAS

1. He joined Arsenal from Celtic for £800,000 in 1983. But which two clubs did he turn down?

2. Which Arsenal bargain-basement cult player vied for a starting place with Nicholas during 1986/87?

3. Whilst at Arsenal he became the subject of tabloid speculation. What nickname was he given by them?

# "YOU'LL NEVER TAKE THE HOME END!" – IV

### A well-known 'Home End' – past or present.
### Name the club it belongs to.

1. Gwladys Street End.

2. The Rookery.

3. Leazes End.


# SOME QUESTIONS ABOUT... DARLINGTON

1. In 2003, which chairman built what is now called the Balfour Webnet Darlington Arena, and named it after himself?

2. In 2002, which two former Newcastle playmakers and international stars – one from England and one from Colombia – did Darlington attempt to lure to Feethams?

3. In January 2007 a young on-loan defender scored on his debut. Having played 15 games, he returned the short distance up the A66 and soon caught the eye of a national coach. Who is he and where did he return to?


# THE 1990s – VIII

1. On November 29th 1998 which debutant replaced Vegard Heggerm in Liverpool's game against Blackburn?

2. In 1995/96 which Plymouth manager personally achieved his fourth play-off victory, having previously been victorious with Notts Co (twice) and Huddersfield?

3. Name the five clubs who won the Football League/Premier League during the 1990s.

## STRIKING FOR GLORY – VIII

### For which clubs and in which season did these deadly duos make defenders lives a misery?

1. John Clayton (31 goals) and Colin Clarke (22 goals).

2. Ted MacDougall (35 goals) and Phil Boyer (15 goals).

3. Imre Varadi (21 goals) and Kevin Keegan (21 goals).

## SOME QUESTIONS ABOUT... HARCHESTER UNITED

1. In December 1992, which 'real life' manager took over at Harchester – was it Barry Fry, Peter Reid or Ron Atkinson?

2. In the turbulent life of The Dragons, the late 1990s were particularly tragic. 1998 saw the chairman die of a heart attack. A year later defender Warren Masters was found dead at his home from carbon monoxide poisoning. In 1999 four players were killed in a plane crash. But what was the fate of skipper John Black following the 1998/99 FA Cup victory over Man Utd?

3. Are Harchester United real?

## FA CUP – VIII

1. Who, in 1901, became the only non-league team to win the FA Cup?

2. In the 1951/52 final, Newcastle fielded the brothers Edward and George Robledo. But which South American country were they originally from – was it Brazil, Uruguay or Chile?

3. Since West Ham won the cup as a Division 2 side in 1979/80, four more clubs from the second tier have reached the final and lost. Name them.

## STARTING XI – V

### From this opening-day-of-the-season starting-eleven, name the club and the season.

Clemence, Stevens, Hughton, Roberts, Miller, Perryman, Chiedozie, Falco, Allen, Hazard, Galvin.


## SOME QUESTIONS ABOUT... BRISTOL CITY

1. What befell City in 1979/80, 1980/81 and 1981/82?

2. In May 1998 City paid £1.2m for this Gillingham striker. A little over a year later they sold him to Wolves for £3.5m. Name him.

3. In 1992 manager Denis Smith signed an Arsenal reject who currently stands as the Premier League's second highest scorer ever. Name him and the price City paid for him?


## AT THE MOVIES – III

### Three plots from football-based movies. Name them.

1. Kilnockie FC are on the road to their first Scottish Cup Final. However their American owner wants to re-locate the club lock, stock and barrel, to Dublin...

2. When England's manager has a heart attack, the search is on for his replacement. The new man goes from being a press and fan favourite, to being one of the most vilified men in the country...

3. A documentary focusing on the seven surviving members of the North Korean team who reached the quarter-final of the 1966 World Cup...

## GETTING THERE – VIII

**Arriving at the railway station, you jump in a cab. This is the route your taxi takes. But which ground are you heading to?**

It's about a mile. Head west and turn left into Neville St then a right into Clayton St West. Turn left at Newgate St and, at the roundabout, take the first exit. Then it's left into Gallowgate. Follow Gallowgate onto Barrack Rd and there it is, on your right.

## SOME QUESTIONS ABOUT... CHELSEA

1. What was the main feature of the Chelsea club badge until manager Ted Drake changed it in 1952?

2. On Boxing Day 1999, what was unique about the team that Gianluca Vialli sent out for a Premier League game at Southampton?

3. Name the three 1970 Chelsea FA Cup winners who have made more appearances for the club than any other players?

## THE 1980s – VIII

1. At the end of 1983/84, who retired as a player whilst with a club he would one-day manage, having helped them gain promotion to Division 1?

2. Which north-east club managed by Brian Little regained their league status at the first attempt after winning the Conference in 1989/90, and which East Anglian club did they replace?

3. On August 28th 1981, three players made their league debuts for Liverpool in a 1-0 defeat away to Wolves. Two were South African – one being born to Australian parents – and the third a Lancashire-born Irishman. Name them.

## THE BIG JOB – III

### Who had the full-time managers job either side of the following appointments?

1. Bournemouth: ___?___ (1980-82) Don Megson (1983) ___?___ (1983-92).

2. Fulham: ___?___ (1996-97) Ray Wilkins (1997-98) ___?___ (1998-99).

3. WBA: ___?___ (1984-85) Ron Saunders (1986-87) ___?___ (1987-88).

## SOME QUESTIONS ABOUT... PETERBOROUGH UNITED

1. Which two future Spurs players made their final appearance for the Posh in a humiliating 5-0 home defeat to Rotherham on Boxing Day 1999?

2. Which Posh player received a surprise call-up to the full England squad for the 2008 friendly games against Trinidad & Tobago and the USA?

3. In their very first Football League season, Posh won the Division 4 title and, in the process, scored a record breaking 134 goals. How many of those goals did Terry Bly contribute – was it 46, 52 or 61?

## HOME OF THE BRAVE – VIII

1. What does the famous Sun headline 'Super Caley Go Ballistic Celtic Are Atrocious' refer to?

2. In the mid-1960s, Celtic's reserve team produced future Scottish internationals Danny McGrain, George Connelly, Lou Macari, David Hay and Kenny Dalglish. What were they known as – was it 'The Bash Street Boys', 'The Minnie Marvels' or 'The Quality Street Kids'?

3. On November 11th 1990, which future Everton legend made his senior debut for Dundee Utd at Rangers?

## SEQUENCES – VIII

### Who is next in the following sequences?

1. USSR, Spain, Italy, ___?___.

2. John Barnes, Kenny Dalglish, Martin O'Neill, ___?___.

3. Geoff Hurst, Martin Peters, Geoff Hurst, ___?___.

## SOME QUESTIONS ABOUT...
## KIDDERMINSTER HARRIERS

1. In 1993/94 Harriers were Conference champions but were refused promotion to the Football League because their ground was not up to the necessary standards. Which club was saved from the drop – was it Northampton, Wigan or Reading?

2. Which honorary 'scouser' led them into the Football League in 1999/2000?

3. The 2006/07 FA Trophy Final between Harriers and Stevenage was the first competitive final to be held at the new Wembley. Apart from becoming the first team to lose there, what other 'first' did Harriers achieve on that day?

## EUROPEAN SILVERWARE – VIII

1. Who are the only British club to appear in five consecutive European Cup-Winners' Cup competitions?

2. In 1971/72 who were the first two clubs to compete in the final of the newly born UEFA Cup?

3. Which manager led Juventus to all three major European trophies between 1977 and 1985?

# HOW MUCH? – VIII

1. Who became the first English £5.5m player in 1991 when he went to Italy?

2. Which Southampton manager signed Senegalese striker Ali Dia, supposedly on the recommendation of former World Player of the Year George Weah, only to discover he had been duped and that Dia had never played professionally?

3. Which 'Mighty Magyar' almost joined Man Utd in 1958 following the Munich air crash – and why didn't it happen?

# SOME QUESTIONS ABOUT... MILLWALL

1. At 11.30am on January 20th 1974, Millwall kicked-off against Fulham at The Den. What was special about this game?

2. Up until the early 1960s, Millwall were still allowed to kick-off their Saturday home games at 3.15pm rather than 3pm. Why?

3. In January 1984 a 17 year-old making his second appearance, scored his very first league goal in a 1-1 draw away to Bournemouth. Name him.

# THE 1970s – VIII

1. On November 28th 1972 it was proposed by the FA Secretary that all under 18s should be banned from the terraces in an effort to curb the on-going problem of hooliganism. Who was this particular official – was it Sir Stanley Rous, Graham Kelly or Dennis Follows?

2. Which club emblazoned the name of a Japanese electronics giant on the front of it's playing shirt in 1979, and thus became the first Football League club to carry shirt sponsorship?

3. On March 1st 1975 which Liverpool-born winger made his debut as a substitute for Willie Morgan in Man Utd's 4-0 victory over Cardiff?

## BY MUTUAL CONSENT? – VIII

### Identify the well-known manager from the following clues.

This busy lower-division midfielder served spireites, millers, monkey hangers, irons, shots, tykes, minstermen and railway men before serving his managerial apprenticeship outside the league with holy blues and brewers. Then he took some seadogs into the league. His ability to take teams up continued with magpies, terriers and pilgrims. After uneventful spells with latics, gulls and shakers, he took over his beloved hometown blades, leading them to both domestic cup semi-finals. But after an eventual relegation he was approached to work his magic at some struggling eagles and took them to the play-offs.

## SOME QUESTIONS ABOUT... REAL MADRID

1. When they won the European Cup for a sixth time in 1965/66, what was unique about the players and coach?

2. Real have won the European Cup/Champions League on nine occasions to date. But how many times have they also carried-off the Spanish domestic title in the same season – is it twice, five times or eight times?

3. In November 2003 who scored their 600th goal in the European Cup/Champions League?

## THE WORLD GAME – VIII

1. When the 17 year-old Pelé appeared in the 1958 World Cup tournament, what squad number was he given?

2. Who is Germany's most capped player with 150 caps?

3. In 1938 The Dutch East Indies became the first Asian team to participate in the World Cup. They played one game, losing 6-0 to Hungary. But what did The Dutch East Indies become following independence in 1945?

## LEAGUE CUP – II

1. The 1962/63 final was contested by arch rivals Birmingham and Aston Villa. In the victorious Birmingham team was a future 'Lisbon Lion'. Was it Bertie Auld, Jimmy Johnstone or Billy McNeill?

2. The 1976/77 final between Aston Villa and Everton went to two replays before Villa eventually came out on top. Where were the three games played?

3. In 1999/2000 which two ex-Irish internationals led their teams out at Wembley for the final?

## SOME QUESTIONS ABOUT... DUNDEE UNITED

1. In 1982/83 United won the Scottish League title under the guidance of Jim McLean. Which future Scottish international boss was his assistant?

2. In the 1960s, like many other clubs, United played summer soccer in the USA. Dundee Utd became Dallas Tornado. But in 1969 what major change to the club occurred as a result of this adventure?

3. On their way to becoming Scotland's first UEFA Cup finalists in 1986/87, United also became the first British team to beat one of Europe's foremost clubs in both a 'home' and 'away' leg. Which club was it?

## BERT TRAUTMANN

1. Which Man C goalkeeping legend did Trautmann replace in 1949?

2. What injury did he suffer in the 1955/56 FA Cup Final victory over Birmingham?

3. What were the first words allegedly said to him on his capture by a British soldier in 1944?
a) "You're nicked, Otto."
b) "Hello Fritz. Fancy a cup of tea?"
c) "Oi, Wolfgang! You're coming back to Blighty with me!"

## SIGN ON THE DOTTED LINE, SON – VIII

### Name the clubs that the following players first signed with as professionals.

1. Terry McDermott.

2. Jimmy Bullard.

3. Teddy Sheringham.

## SOME QUESTIONS ABOUT... YORK CITY

1. In 1954/55 York reached the semi-final of the FA Cup where they lost in a replay to eventual winners Newcastle. What division were they in at the time?

2. Which controversial journalist, biographer, diarist, broadcaster and midfield player made his Football League debut with the Minstermen in 1965?

3. In 1968/69 a prolific strike partnership came together at Bootham Crescent, which would go on to cause havoc for Bournemouth, Norwich and Southampton. Name them.

## THE 1960s – VIII

1. In 1968/69 which club completed its four-year return journey, which involved three relegations, from Division 1 to Division 4?

2. Which 27 year-old 'double' winning Spurs and Scotland midfielder was tragically killed in 1964 when he was struck by lightening whilst sheltering under a tree during a round of golf?

3. On September 1st 1962 two international footballers were born. One was a Kent-born Republic of Ireland international striker, the other was the Amsterdam-born son of an Afro-Surinamese migrant. Name them.

## OLD GROUNDS FOR NEW – IV

### Which clubs used to play their home games at the following grounds?

1. Victoria Ground.

2. Springfield Park.

3. Manor Ground.

## SOME QUESTIONS ABOUT... ROCHDALE

1. Which brother of, and uncle to a famous north-east football dynasty played full-back for Rochdale against Norwich in the 1961.62 League Cup Final?

2. One half of a popular Lancashire comedy double-act became chairman of Rochdale in the mid-1980s. Who was it?

3. When did Rochdale last play outside the Football League's basement division – was it 1965/66, 1973/74 or have they always played in the basement division?

## THREE LIONS – VIII

1. How did England qualify for the 1966 and 1970 World Cup tournament?

2. In 1975 England beat Cyprus 5-0 in a Euro Championship qualifier at Wembley. Which former Fulham full-back scored all five goals?

3. Which two former England managers were born in the North-East of England?

## STAT-TASTIC – VIII

### Identify the player from the following career statistics.

Born: Welwyn Garden City.
League Career Span: 1989/90 to the present.
International Caps: 39 apps – 0 goals (to date).

| CLUB/NICKNAME | LEAGUE APPS | GOALS |
|---|---|---|
| Hornets | 89 | 0 |
| Reds | 216 | 0 |
| Villans | 67 | 0 |
| Hammers | 91 | 0 |
| Citizens | 93 | 0 |
| Pompey (to date) | 73 | 0 |

## SOME QUESTIONS ABOUT... NORWICH CITY

1. In January 2006 Dean Ashton went to West Ham for upwards of £7m. But who was bought from WBA a week later to replace him?

2. Which welsh-born former goalkeeper managed them to victory over Bayern Munich in the 1993/94 UEFA Cup 2nd Round?

3. Which World Cup winner was Norwich Player of the Year in 1975/76 and 1976/77?

## BOBBY MOORE

1. Which fedora wearing, cigar smoking defender was Moore's mentor and predecessor in the No. 6 shirt at West Ham?

2. Who was Moore negotiating to join, prior to the 1966 World Cup triumph?

3. Moore won his 108th and final cap in a single goal defeat in November 1973. Who were the opponents and who scored the only goal?

## WHAT'S THAT ON THE FRONT OF YOUR SHIRT? – II

### Shirt sponsors over the years. Name the clubs.

1. ' Fosters Lager' – 'Coleman's' – 'flybe.com'.

2. 'Peugeot' – 'Subaru' – 'Cassidy Group'.

3. 'Gulf Air' – 'Coors' – 'Fly Emirates'.


## SOME QUESTIONS ABOUT... FEYENOORD

1. In the 1969/70 European Cup Final, which British club did they beat to become Holland's first winners of the trophy?

2. Which former West Ham and Bermudan international turned out for Feyenoord in 1977/78?

3. In the 1970 World Club Championship, Feyenoord drew 2-2 against Estudiantes in Buenos Aires. The Dutch won the return leg 1-0 with a goal by Joop van Daele. But what did van Daele have broken by a frustrated defender immediately after he scored – was it his arm, his big toe or his glasses?


## PRE-1960s – VIII

1. Five future managers were part of a legendary 1950s 'Academy' of West Ham players who would sit in the Cafe Cassettari near to Upton Park, discussing the finer points of football. Name them.

2. Two of the five club stadiums that England used for 'home' games between 1950 and 1959 no longer exist. Name them.

3. Which manager, who took France to the 1982 World Cup semi-finals before leading them to victory in Euro '84, played and scored for Stade de Reims in the very first European Cup Final against Real Madrid in 1955/56 – was it Just Fontaine, Michel Hidalgo or Henri Michel?

## 1966 AND ALL THAT – V

1. When German referee Rudolf Kreitlein sent-off Argentine captain Antonio Rattin in the quarter-final against England, what explanation did he give for the dismissal?
a) Rattin had used foul and abusive language to him.
b) He didn't like the way Rattin had looked at him.
c) Rattin would not accept that he was wrong to keep protesting.

2. With which clubs did the eleven World Cup winners – Banks, Cohen, Wilson, Stiles, J. Charlton, Moore, Ball, Hunt, B. Charlton, Hurst and Peters – finish their Football League careers?

3. Which two nations were appearing in their first World Cup finals?

## SOME QUESTIONS ABOUT... PORTUGAL

1. In the four Euro Championships Portugal have qualified for, how many times have they reached the quarter-finals?

2. The legendary striker Eusébio was known as 'The Black Panther', or 'The Black Pearl'. But in which Portuguese colony was he born – was it Cape Verde, Mozambique or Angola?

3. Which player has won a record 127 caps and scored 32 goals for Portugal?

## EURO CHAMPIONSHIPS – VIII

1. In the preliminary round of Euro '64, who refused to play Albania because the two countries had officially been at war since 1912 – was it Greece, Italy or Turkey?

2. When Denmark beat Holland 5-4 on penalties to reach the Euro '92 Final, who was the only Dutchman to miss his spot-kick?

3. Name the two 1976 Dutch squad-members who were playing for Barcelona at the time?

## INTO THE LEAGUE! – IV

### Guess the club from the details of their first ever home league game.

OPPOSITION: Wolves.
LEAGUE: Division 4.
DATE: August 15th 1987.
HOME GROUND: Athletic Ground, Seamer Road.
COLOURS: All red.

## SOME QUESTIONS ABOUT... EXETER CITY

1. Which national team played its first ever game against a touring Exeter team in July 1914 – was it Argentina, Italy or Brazil?

2. In 1934/35 Exeter beat Aldershot 8-1 in a Division 3 (South) game. But what was the half-time score?

3. Name two England captains who have managed Exeter.

## TODAY'S THE DAY – VIII

### Identify the major news story that occurred on the day when the following events were happening in the world of football.

Five months before The News of the World break the story of English football's greatest betting scandal, recently retired Mansfield inside-forward Jimmy Gauld is found guilty of offering bribes to players and fined £60. In an effort to curb growing hooliganism Everton erect scaffold barriers behind their goals. Going into the weekend fixtures, Sheff Utd top the league and Sunderland lead Division 2. Tranmere goalkeeper Harry Leyland is suspended for fourteen days after kicking a Stockport opponent two weeks earlier. Meanwhile in Dallas, Texas...

# ANSWERS

**ME! ME! ME! – I**
Augustus Cassius (Gus) Caesar. Born Tottenham. Played for Arsenal, QPR (loan), Cambridge Utd, Bristol C, Airdrie and Colchester. Nick Hornby wrote about him in 'Fever Pitch'.

**SOME ANSWERS ABOUT... EVERTON**
1. The Everton Mint.
2. Football League Championship and European Cup-Winners' Cup.
3. Brazil.

**THE 2000s – I**
1. They all lost to Liverpool in major finals. Birmingham (League Cup), Arsenal (FA Cup) and Alavés (UEFA Cup).
2. He introduced red and yellow cards. Aston based the idea on traffic lights.
3. The Queen.

**PRAWN SANDWICH ANYONE? – I**
1. Liverpool (de Burgh) v Darlington (Reeves).
2. Bristol C (Robinson) v Southend (Moyet).
3. Chesterfield (Benn) v Stockport (Yarwood).

**SOME ANSWERS ABOUT... ROTHERHAM UNITED**
1. Goal average. They finished equal on points with champions Birmingham and runners-up Luton.
2. Aston Villa.
3. Shaun Goater.

**WORLD CUP – I**
1. None at all.
2. Domingo, Carreras and Pavarotti began their collaboration as 'The Three Tenors' with a concert held in Rome.
3. The 1974 World Cup Final between W. Germany and Holland, and also the Euro '88 Final where the Dutch played the Soviet Union.

**HE SAID WHAT? – I**
1. Johan Cruyff.
2. Brian Clough.
3. Bob Paisley.

**SOME ANSWERS ABOUT... QUEENS PARK RANGERS**
1. Formula One supremo Bernie Ecclestone and Renault F1 boss Flavio Briatore.
2. The League Cup and Division 3 Championship.
3. Terry Venables, Frank Sibley, Trevor Francis, Gerry Francis, Ray Wilkins, Ian Holloway, Gary Waddock and John Gregory.

**STUART PEARCE**
1. Ian Butterworth.
2. A toy horse called Beanie that belonged to his 7 year-old daughter.
3. His services as an electrician – just in case the football career didn't work out.

### STAT-TASTIC! – I
Peter Crouch: Spurs, Dulwich Hamlet, IFK Hässleholm, QPR, Portsmouth, Aston Villa, Norwich , Southampton, Liverpool, Portsmouth.

### SOME ANSWERS ABOUT... AC MILAN
1. Inter Milan.
2. Cricket. Originally founded as the Milan Cricket and Football Club.
3. Coach Arrigo Sacchi signed Marco van Basten, Ruud Gullit and Frank Rijkaard.

### THE 1990s – I
1. Michael Owen (Liverpool). His debut goal was at Wimbledon, and the legendary strike was against Argentina (World Cup '88).
2. Notts Co.
3. Osvaldo Ardiles (Spurs), Mike Walker (Everton) and Ron Atkinson (Aston Villa).

### STRIKING FOR GLORY – I
1. Bristol R (1973/74).
2. Colchester (2006/07).
3. Crystal Palace (1987/88).

### SOME ANSWERS ABOUT... STOKE CITY
1. 1984/85.
2. Stoke.
3. Gordon Banks, Geoff Hurst and unused squad member George Eastham.

### THE FA CUP – I
1. Arsenal and Man Utd.
2. Ron Atkinson.
3. Wimbledon (1987/88).

### WHO'S MISSING? – I
Alex Stepney, Nobby Stiles and David Sadler.

### SOME ANSWERS ABOUT... WIGAN ATHLETIC
1. The Scottish League Division 2.
2. Southport.
3. 10 seasons.

### STANLEY MATTHEWS
1. Port Vale.
2. 46 years-old. Stoke won the Division 2 title the following season.
3. Beneath the centre circle at Stoke's Britannia Stadium.

### GETTING THERE... – I
Kenilworth Rd, Luton.

### SOME ANSWERS ABOUT...MIDDLESBROUGH
1. Malcolm Crosby.
2. Brian Clough.
3. Harold Shepherdson, Bryan Robson and Steve McClaren.

### THE 1980s – I
1. Three points for a win.
2. Lord Justice Taylor of Gosforth. (The Taylor Report).
3. John Toshack.

**THE BIG JOB – I**
1. Don Howe (1984-86) Graham (86-95) Bruce Rioch (1995-96).
2. Allan Clarke (1980-82) Gray (82-85) Billy Bremner (1985-88).
3. Bobby Charlton (1973-75) Catterick (75-77) Nobby Stiles (1977-81).

**SOME ANSWERS ABOUT... BURY**
1. Lee Dixon. He had previously played for Burnley and Chester.
2. FC United of Manchester.
3. Peter Reid.

**HOME OF THE BRAVE – I**
1. Aberdeen and Dundee Utd.
2. Gordon Smith.
3. Third Lanark.

**SEQUENCES – I**
1. Steve McClaren (Middlesbrough managers).
2. Chelsea (Premier League runners-up).
3. Billy Bremner of Leeds (FA Cup winning captains).

**SOME ANSWERS ABOUT... CELTIC**
1. Scottish League, Scottish Cup, Scottish League Cup and European Cup. They also won the once hotly contested Glasgow Cup.
2. Gil Scott-Heron. He is considered to be one of the founding fathers of rap music.
3. 7 years. Their previous success had been the Scottish League Cup in 1958.

**EUROPEAN SILVERWARE – I**
1. Parc des Princes, Paris.
2. Rangers (1972) and Aberdeen (1983).
3. The Inter-Cities Fairs Cup.

**BY MUTUAL CONSENT... – I**
Howard Wilkinson. Played for Sheff Utd, Sheff Wed, Brighton and Boston. Managed Boston, Notts Co, Sheff Wed, Leeds and Sunderland. Worked as FA Technical Director as well as chairman of the League Managers Association. He was caretaker manager of England on two occasions.

**SOME ANSWERS ABOUT... BIRMINGHAM CITY**
1. 1943.
2. The Inter-Cities Fairs Cup Final. They lost both to Barcelona and Roma respectively.
3. Trevor Francis. The official figure was allegedly £999,999. Forest boss Brian Clough didn't want the £1m figure going to the player's head.

**THE 1970s – I**
1. Barrow were replaced by Hereford.
2. Ian Rush (Chester).
3. Lincoln.

Page 17

**HOW MUCH? – I**

1. £46m.

2. Jean-Marc Bosman from Belgium.

3. Alf Common. He moved from Sunderland to Middlesbrough.

**SOME ANSWERS ABOUT... BLACKPOOL**

1. Preston.

2. Three. (Lost in 1948 and 1951, and famously beat Bolton in 1953).

3. Sam Allardyce.

**THE WORLD GAME – I**

1. The European Cup and the Copa Libertadores.

2. FC Cologne.

3. Juventus, A.C. Milan, Fiorentina, Lazio, and Reggina.

Page 18

**ANOTHER BITE AT THE CHERRY? – I**

Steve Finnan, Jamie Carragher, Xabi Alonso, Steven Gerrard, John Arne Riise, Harry Kewell.

**SOME ANSWERS ABOUT... READING**

1. Huntley & Palmer.

2. 13.

3. Robin Friday.

**JACK'S REPUBLIC**

1. Pat Bonner (Celtic) and Paul McGrath (Aston Villa).

2. Eventual finalists Italy 1-0 with a goal by Ray Houghton.

3. David O'Leary.

Page 19

**SIGN ON THE DOTTED LINE, SON – I**

1. Norwich.

2. Man Utd.

3. Reading.

**SOME ANSWERS ABOUT... QUEENS PARK, GLASGOW**

1. All eleven.

2. Twice.

3. Egypt.

**THE 1960s – I**

1. 1960/61.

2. 16th.

3. The League and the FA Cup.

Page 20

**BIRTH OF A CLUB**

Gillingham.

**SOME ANSWERS ABOUT... SPAIN**

1. Spain beat England 4-3 in Madrid.

2. José Luis Aragonés. 'Zapatones' means Big Boots. He was a free-kick specialist.

3. Hungary.

**THREE LIONS – I**
1. 34.
2. France in World Cup '82.
3. Robson (Fulham), McClaren (Oxford), Revie (Leeds), Taylor (Lincoln) and Venables (Crystal Palace).

Page 21

**LATIN HOMEWORK – I**
1. Everton – Nothing But The Best Will Do.
2. Stoke – Unity in Strength.
3. Cheltenham – Health and Learning.
**SOME ANSWERS ABOUT... SHAMROCK ROVERS**
1. Man Utd.
2. Tolka Park.
3. John Aldridge.
**DIDIER DROGBA**
1. Le Mans.
2. Tito.
3. Sheff Utd, Celtic and Birmingham.

Page 22

**INTO THE LEAGUE! – I**
Grimsby.
**SOME ANSWERS ABOUT... MANCHESTER UNITED**
1. Yes. On the same day Birmingham confirmed their safety by beating already relegated Norwich. Even if United had won against City and also won their final game against Stoke two days later, they still would have been one point shy of safety.
2. Mark Hughes (Blackburn), Roy Keane (Sunderland), Steve Bruce (Wigan), Darren Ferguson (Peterborough), Mark Robins (Rotherham), Simon Davies (Chester) and Paul Ince (MK Dons).
3. Lou Macari.
**PRE-1960s – I**
1. Paul McGrath.
2. Merthyr Town.
3. Fulham (Division 1) and QPR (Division 2).

Page 23

**1966 AND ALL THAT – I**
1. West Germany.
2. Goodison Park.
3. Pickles.
**SOME ANSWERS ABOUT... ALDERSHOT TOWN**
1. Teddy Sheringham.
2. 15 seasons.
3. Gary Waddock.
**EURO CHAMPIONSHIPS – I**
1. Kevin Keegan (Hamburg) and Tony Woodcock (FC Cologne).
2. Born in Germany, he became the only victorious manager born outside the country he led.
3. France were hosts. After qualification, only four countries actually played in a tournament comprising of a semi-final, a final and a third-place play-off.

**ODD ONE OUT – I**
Crystal Palace. He signed for them in 1988 but never made an appearance.
**SOME ANSWERS ABOUT... WYCOMBE WANDERERS**
1. Furniture making.
2. 2000/01 (FA Cup) and 2006/07 (League Cup).
3. Martin O'Neill.
**TODAY'S THE DAY – I**
September 11th 2001. Terrorists attack the World Trade Centre and The Pentagon.

**MEI MEI MEI – II**
Peter Shilton. Played for Leicester, Stoke, Nott'm Forest, Southampton, Derby, Plymouth [player/manager], Bolton, Coventry, West Ham and Leyton Orient.
**SOME ANSWERS ABOUT... HULL CITY**
1. N. Ireland.
2. Scunthorpe.
3. All black.
**THE 2000s – II**
1. They became the first former winners of a major trophy to play at this level, having won the League Cup in 1986.
2. Six. Three players had been sent-off and, with all substitutes used, two further players limped off injured. The rules state that each team must be fielding at least 7 players each.
3. Coventry (Ricoh Arena) and Swansea (Liberty Stadium).

**STARTING XI – I**
QPR (1972/73).
**SOME ANSWERS ABOUT... HIBERNIAN**
1. Ireland.
2. Blyton created 'The Famous Five' children's adventures. This forward line, arguably the best in the history of Scottish football, became known as 'The Famous Five'.
3. Stranraer.
**WORLD CUP – II**
1. Egypt. They gained no votes.
2. French. He was President of FIFA.
3. Both saw victory for Brazil over Italy.

**HE SAID WHAT? – II**
1. Joey Barton.
2. Eric Cantona.
3. Gordon Strachan.
**SOME ANSWERS ABOUT... PORTSMOUTH**
1. Alexandria, Egypt.
2. Jim Smith.
3. Jimmy Dickinson in 1954.

**ROY KEANE**
1. Steve Hodge.
2. Blackburn.
3. Eric Cantona.

Page 28

**"YOU'LL NEVER TAKE THE HOME END!" – I**
1. Craven Cottage, Fulham.
2. City Ground, Nott'm Forest.
3. Highbury, Arsenal.

**SOME ANSWERS ABOUT... AJAX OF AMSTERDAM**
1. To keep the trophy, having won it three times in succession.
2. The Twelve Apostles.
3. Vic Buckingham.

**THE 1990s – II**
1. Five. (Frank Burrows, Bobby Smith, Jimmy Rimmer, Kevin Cullis and Jan Molby).
2. Sheff Wed. Alan Shearer scored five.
3. Leeds were champions and Sheff Wed finished third.

Page 29

**STRIKING FOR GLORY – II**
1. They have all scored goals in three separate Euro Championship tournaments.
2. Davies (Southampton), Gould (Coventry), Marsh (QPR) and Phythain (Hartlepools Utd).
3. David Beckham (1998, 2002 and 2006).

**SOME ANSWERS ABOUT... BARNSLEY**
1. Crystal Palace.
2. Tommy Taylor.
3. N. Ireland.

**FA CUP – II**
1. Barnsley and WBA.
2. Stuart McCall.
3. In 1872 he scored the first FA Cup Final goal for Wanderers against Royal Engineers.

Page 30

**CUP FINAL COLOURS – I**
1.White shirts, white shorts and red socks.
2. Yellow and black striped shirts, black shorts and yellow socks.
3. Bottle-green and white quartered shirts, bottle green shorts and white socks.

**SOME ANSWERS ABOUT... CARDIFF CITY**
1. Cricket.
2. Wales v England.
3. John Toshack.

**ALLY'S TARTAN ARMY**
1. Hampden Park. An estimated 25,000 people were there to cheer them on their way.
2. "Retain it".
3. Willie Johnston.

**GETTING THERE – II**
Molineux, Wolves.
**SOME ANSWERS ABOUT... OXFORD UNITED**
1. Headington Utd.
2. Thames Valley Royals. Jim Smith, the Oxford boss at the time, would have been manager.
3. Dean Windass.
**THE 1980s – II**
1. The Bradford City fire and the Heysel Stadium disaster.
2. Alan Smith and Michael Thomas.
3. Burnley and Bolton.

**NET MINDERS – I**
Keelan (Norwich), Godden (WBA), Roche (Man Utd), Bonetti (Chelsea), Daines (Spurs), Parkes (QPR), Rimmer (Aston Villa), Cooper (Ipswich), Shilton (Nott'm Forest), Bradshaw (Wolves), Corrigan (Man C), Shaw (Bristol C), Sealey (Coventry), Jennings (Arsenal), Stewart (Middlesbrough), Montgomery (Birmingham), Wells (Southampton), Middleton (Derby), Clemence (Liverpool), McDonagh (Bolton), Wood (Everton), Harvey (Leeds).
**SOME ANSWERS ABOUT... BLACKBURN ROVERS**
1. Aston Villa and Everton.
2. Dave Whelan.
3. Sven-Göran Eriksson.
**HOME OF THE BRAVE – II**
1. 101,000.
2. The Wembley Wizards.
3. Sevilla and Espanyol. Sevilla won 3-1 on penalties after a 2-2 draw.

**SEQUENCES – II**
1. Plymouth (Runners-up in Division 3 (South) every season from 1921/22 to 1926/27).
2. Fabio Capello (They preceded him as coach of Real Madrid).
3. Leicester (The first four winners of the League Cup).
**SOME ANSWERS ABOUT... DAGENHAM & REDBRIDGE**
1. Dagenham (FA Trophy), Leytonstone, Ilford and Walthamstow Ave (FA Amateur Cup).
2. Colchester and Southend.
3. Isthmian League.
**EUROPEAN SILVERWARE – II**
1. Frank Lampard, Joe Cole, Michael Carrick, Carlos Tevez and Rio Ferdinand.
2. Paolo Maldini (AC Milan).
3. AC Milan (1963), Man Utd (1968), Ajax (1971), Liverpool (1978) and Barcelona (1992).

**BY MUTUAL CONSENT? – II**
David Moyes. Played for Celtic, Cambridge Utd, Bristol C, Shrewsbury, Dunfermline and Hamilton. Player/manager at Preston before hanging-up his boots. Then Everton.

**SOME ANSWERS ABOUT... WORKINGTON**
1. New Brighton.
2. Bill Shankly.
3. Scott Carson.
**THE 1970s – II**
1. Bolton, Notts Co and Blackburn.
2. Clive Allen.
3. Don Howe.

Page 35

**WHAT'S IN A NICKNAME? – I**
Scunthorpe. 'The Iron'.
**SOME ANSWERS ABOUT... BRISTOL ROVERS**
1. Twerton Park, Bath.
2. They wore black and played next door to the Arab Rugby Club.
3. Gerry Francis.
**THE WORLD GAME – II**
1. Gérard Houllier (Liverpool) and Jacques Santini (Spurs).
2. Stefan Kovács.
3. Ernst Happel.

Page 36

**HOW MUCH? – II**
1. Martin Peters (West Ham to Spurs). Jimmy Greaves travelled the other way.
2. Asa Hartford.
3. Inter Milan.
**SOME ANSWERS ABOUT... MANCHESTER CITY**
1. Colin Bell.
2. Huddersfield (10-1).
3. Fulham and Liverpool.
**KENNY DALGLISH**
1. Rangers.
2. For the first time in twelve years Celtic were trophy-less.
3. Denis Law.

Page 37

**SIGN ON THE DOTTED LINE, SON... – II**
1. Luton.
2. Notts Co.
3. Monaco.
**SOME ANSWERS ABOUT... ACCRINGTON**
1. 1968.
2. All the other clubs are still competing in the Premier League or Football League.
(Aston Villa, Blackburn, Bolton, Burnley, Derby, Everton, Notts Co, Preston, Stoke,
WBA and Wolves).
3. Oxford.
**THE 1960s – II**
1. Gianfraco Zola.
2. c) "I think I've found you a genius."
3. They were relegated from Division 1.

**MR CHAIRMAN – I**
1. Stan Flashman (Barnet).
2. Alan Sugar (Spurs).
3. Firoz Kassam (Oxford).

**SOME ANSWERS ABOUT... GILLINGHAM**
1. Ipswich. They regained their league status in 1950/51.
2. Man C.
3. Brent Sancho (Trinidad and Tobago) in 2006.

**THREE LIONS – II**
1. Ireland 0 – 13 England.
2. Alf Ramsey and Terry Venables.
3. David Seaman (75 caps).

**STAT-TASTIC – II**
Martin Keown: Arsenal, Brighton, Aston Villa, Everton, Arsenal, Leicester, Reading

**SOME ANSWERS ABOUT... CARLISLE UNITED**
1. Aldershot.
2. Bill Shankly.
3. Premier League football within ten years.

**JIMMY GREAVES**
1. Newcastle.
2. Barnet.
3. Ian St John.

**STARTING XI – II**
Newcastle (1996/97).

**SOME ANSWERS ABOUT... SUNDERLAND**
1. Win the League Championship wearing striped shirts.
2. Southampton (1976) and West Ham (1980).
3. Ex-midfielder Kevin Ball followed by club chairman Niall Quinn.

**PRE-1960s – II**
1. Notts Co and Nott'm Forest.
2. b) The game, as played by women, was distasteful.
3. Division 3 (South). Ipswich finished top and Norwich finished bottom.

**EURO '96 AND ALL THAT... – I**
1. The Republic of Ireland and Holland. The Dutch won 2-0.
2. Scotland would have qualified for the knock-out stages with a superior goal difference.
3. At the time, every member of their squads played their domestic football on 'home' soil.

**SOME ANSWERS ABOUT... RUSHDEN & DIAMONDS**
1. Max Griggs owned Dr Marten's.
2. Brian Talbot.
3. Model owls.

**EURO CHAMPIONSHIPS II**
1. Portugal and Greece – the same as the final. Greece won both.
2. Luxembourg.
3. a) carré magique (magic square).

Page 42

**OLD GROUNDS FOR NEW – I**
1. Bristol R.
2. Scunthorpe.
3. Walsall.
**SOME ANSWERS ABOUT... HEREFORD UNITED**
1. John Charles.
2. West Ham.
3. One (1976/77).
**TODAY'S THE DAY – II**
November 26th 1976. Middle England panics as The Sex Pistols release 'Anarchy in the UK'.

Page 43

**ANOTHER BITE AT THE CHERRY? – II**
Bobby Moore, Alan Ball, Bobby Charlton, Geoff Hurst and Martin Peters.
**SOME ANSWERS ABOUT... ABERDEEN**
1. Alex Ferguson.
2. Dugouts.
3. Alex McLeish (Birmingham), Gordon Strachan (Celtic) and Mark McGhee (Motherwell).
**THE 2000s – III**
1. Sheff Wed.
2. It was the 500,000th goal in the history of English league football.
3. Harry Redknapp. (Portsmouth to Southampton).

Page 44

**TAKING THE MIC – I**
John Motson.
**SOME ANSWERS ABOUT... MACCLESFIELD TOWN**
1. The FA Trophy.
2. Germany.
3. Sammy McIlroy.
**WORLD CUP – III**
1. 56 seconds.
2. Turkey and co-hosts South Korea. Turkey won 3-2.
3. Italy had snubbed the first World Cup tournament, which Uruguay hosted.

Page 45

**HE SAID WHAT? – III**
1. Gary Lineker.
2. Kenneth Wolstenholme (commentating on a Bobby Charlton goal).
3. Harry Redknapp.
**SOME ANSWERS ABOUT... NORTHAMPTON TOWN**
1. Northamptonshire County Cricket Club.
2. Herbert Chapman.
3. Six. They went from Division 4 to Division 1 and back again.

**WAYNE ROONEY**
1. Duncan Ferguson.
2. '18'.
3. Ricardo Carvalho.

Page 46

**AT THE MOVIES – I**
1. Escape to Victory (1980).
2. Zidane, A 21st Century Portrait (2006).
3. The Arsenal Stadium Mystery (1940).
**SOME ANSWERS ABOUT... BRADFORD PARK AVENUE**
1. Cambridge Utd.
2. Ron Greenwood.
3. He had played for Celtic.
**THE 1990s – III**
1. Chris Waddle (Sheff Wed).
2. Swindon.
3. Dr Jozef Vengloš at Aston Villa. (Doctorate in Physical Education).

Page 47

**STRIKING FOR GLORY – III**
1. Joe Jordan (4 goals).
2. Rangers (355 goals).
3. Gabriel Batistuta.
**SOME ANSWERS ABOUT... NEWCASTLE UNITED**
1. One.
2. Alan Shearer and Jackie Milburn.
3. Frank Clark. (Nott'm Forest).
**FA CUP – III**
1. Gretna in 2nd Qualifying Round in 2001/02.
2. Old Trafford, Manchester.
3. Teddy Sheringham.

Page 48

**LEAGUE CUP – I**
1. Stoke (Victoria Ground), and Leicester (Filbert St).
2. Rochdale.
3. 1980/81.
**SOME ANSWERS ABOUT... SOUTHEND UNITED**
1. Freddy Eastwood.
2. Peter Taylor.
3. Bobby Moore.
**BINGHAM'S BOYS**
1. Jimmy Nicholl.
2. Armstrong (Watford), Hamilton (Burnley), Whiteside (Man Utd) and Clarke (Bournemouth).
3. Martin O'Neill (1982) and Sammy McIlroy (1986).

Page 49

**GETTING THERE – III**
Turf Moor, Burnley.

**SOME ANSWERS ABOUT... WIMBLEDON**
1. They became the only club to win both top domestic trophies at amateur and professional level. They had won the FA Amateur Cup in 1963.
2. A camel.
3. Dave Bassett.
**THE 1980s – III**
1. Harry Gregg.
2. Bristol C and Bristol R.
3. Joe Royle and Graeme Sharp.

Page 50

**ME! ME! ME! – III**
Stan Bowles. Played for Man C, Bury, Crewe, Carlisle, QPR (replacing Rodney Marsh), Nott'm Forest, Leyton Orient and Brentford. Played for England under Ramsey, Mercer and Revie.
**SOME ANSWERS ABOUT... SCARBOROUGH**
1. Wigan.
2. Neil Warnock.
3. 'The Theatre of Chips'.
**HOME OF THE BRAVE – III**
1. 1992. Also with Rangers.
2. Andy Roxburgh and Alex Ferguson.
3. Nine.

Page 51

**SEQUENCES – III**
1. Cardiff. (Losing FA Cup finalists 2004/05 to 2007/08).
2. Aldershot. (Conference champions 2004/05 to 2007/08).
3. Alex Ferguson. (Man Utd managers).
**SOME ANSWERS ABOUT... TOTTENHAM HOTSPUR**
1. Inter-Cities Fairs Cup.
2. 50/51 (Division 1)  60/61 (League and Cup 'double') 70/71 (League Cup) 80/81 (FA Cup) and 90/91 (FA Cup).
3. Arthur Rowe.
**EUROPEAN SILVERWARE – III**
1. Vladimir Ilyich Lenin. (The Grand Arena of the Central Lenin Stadium)
2. Anderlecht.
3. Liverpool.

Page 52

**PRAWN SANDWICH ANYONE? – II**
1. Arsenal (Lucas) v Charlton (Davidson).
2. Dundee Utd (Kelly) v Rangers (Smillie).
3. AFC Wimbledon (Armstrong) v Watford (Halliwell).
**SOME ANSWERS ABOUT... CAMBRIDGE UNITED**
1. Abbey United.
2. John Beck.
3. Claude Le Roy.
**THE 1970s – III**
1. Alex Stepney.
2. Ipswich (1960/61 and 1961/62).
3. QPR. They finished one point behind the champions.

**BY MUTUAL CONSENT? – III**
Giovanni Trapattoni. Played for AC Milan. Managed AC Milan, Juventus (twice), Inter Milan, Bayern Munich (twice), Cagliari, Fiorentina, Italy, Benfica, VfB Stuttgart, Red Bull Salzburg and the Republic of Ireland.

**SOME ANSWERS ABOUT... PLYMOUTH ARGYLE**
1. Bristol C (116 miles) and Norwich (358 miles).
2. Peter Shilton.
3. Man Utd. (Ordered to play the game at least 300km from home following crowd trouble).

**FRANCO BARESI**
1. AC Milan.
2. Fulham.
3. Inter Milan.

**WHO'S MISSING – II**
Eddie McCreadie, Billy Bremner and Denis Law.

**SOME ANSWERS ABOUT... GLASGOW RANGERS**
1. Mo Johnston. It was alleged that Rangers had an 'unwritten policy' of not signing Catholics.
2. Dick Advocaat and Paul Le Guen.
3. Dumbarton.

**THE WORLD GAME – III**
1. Sweden.
2. Nott'm Forest.
3. Real Madrid and Barcelona.

**BENCHWARMING – I**
1. Man Utd v Aston Villa (Division 1).
2. Bristol C v Swindon. (Division 3).
3. Sheff Wed v Wimbledon. (Division 1).

**SOME ANSWERS ABOUT... HALIFAX TOWN**
1. Alan Ball Snr.
2. 36,885.
3. Be relegated to the Conference twice.

**THE 1960s – III**
1. Come on as a substitute in a Football League match.
2. Next to bottom of Division 4.
3. Alf Ramsey was offered the England manager's job, which he accepted.

**SIGN ON THE DOTTED LINE, SON – III**
1. Man Utd.
2. Wimbledon.
3. Leeds.

**SOME ANSWERS ABOUT... WEST HAM UNITED**
1. Thames Ironworks.
2. Sol Campbell and John Terry.
3. Ray Wilson (Everton). The sculpture was based on an original photograph.

**THREE LIONS – III**
1. Peter Taylor (Crystal Palace).
2. Alf Ramsey and Bobby Robson both managed Ipswich.
3. Robson, G. Taylor, Venables, Hoddle, Wilkinson, Keegan and Eriksson.

Page 57

**STAT-TASTIC – III**
Robbie Keane: Wolves, Coventry, Inter Milan, Leeds, Spurs & Liverpool.
**SOME ANSWERS ABOUT... FULCHESTER UNITED**
1. Billy Thompson (Billy the Fish).
2. Owner and chairman.
3. Robert Maxwell.
**IAN CALLAGHAN**
1. Most league appearances. (640 between 1960 and 1978).
2. John Toshack for Swansea.
3. Once.

Page 58

**INTO THE LEAGUE! – II**
Sunderland.
**SOME ANSWERS ABOUT... FRANCE**
1. Michel Platini. They lost to W. Germany.
2. Parc des Princes (Paris), La Beaujoire (Nantes), Stade Geoffroy-Guichard (St Etienne) and Stade Vélodrome (Marseille).
3. Stade de Reims.
**PRE-1960s – III**
1. 1971.
2. 15 years & 5 months.
3. Under soil heating.

Page 59

**1966 AND ALL THAT... – II**
1. England, Brazil, W. Germany and Italy.
2. Tuesday August 2nd at Wembley Stadium, kicking off at 7.30.
3. Gordon Banks (Chesterfield) and Ray Wilson (Huddersfield).
**SOME ANSWERS ABOUT... MORECAMBE**
1. Sammy McIlroy.
2. Layer Road, Colchester (6,320).
3. Ipswich.
**EURO CHAMPIONSHIPS – III**
1. Glenn Hoddle and Mark Hateley.
2. Lost 3-2 to both Portugal and Rumania.
3. A penalty shoot-out. It was the first in a major international tournament. Germany lost.

Page 60

**HOW MUCH? – III**
1. £0.5m.
2. Sheff Wed.
3. Denis Law and Allan Clarke.

**SOME ANSWERS ABOUT... WEST BROMWICH ALBION**
1. Division 2 (3rd Tier) Play-Off Final.
2. Promotion to Division 1 and the FA Cup.
3. Tony Brown.
**TODAY'S THE DAY – III**
February 6th 1952. Princess Elizabeth is told of her succession to the throne following the death of her father King George VI.

**ME! ME! ME! – IV**
Ashley Cole. He has played for Arsenal, Crystal Palace (loan) and Chelsea.
**SOME ANSWERS ABOUT... CHELTENHAM TOWN**
1. Steve Cotterill.
2. Nine.
3. Bobby Gould.
**THE 2000s – IV**
1. FC United of Manchester.
2. Ronnie Moore.
3. 12 games.

**REBRANDING TIME**
1. Watford.
2. Brighton.
3. Colchester.
**SOME ANSWERS ABOUT... SOUTHAMPTON**
1. Martin Chivers.
2. Martin Peters.
3. Bobby Stokes, Ted Bates, Matthew Le Tissier, Danny/Rod Wallace and Mick Channon.
**WORLD CUP – IV**
1. Zinedine Zidane (France) butted Marco Materazzi (Italy) and was sent off.
2. Because FIFA would not allow them to play barefoot.
3. 1974 in W. Germany.

**SKIPPER! – I**
1. Coventry v Spurs (1986/87 FA Cup Final).
2. Celtic v Inter Milan (1966/67 European Cup Final).
3. Brazil v Germany (2002 World Cup Final).
**SOME ANSWERS ABOUT... STOCKPORT COUNTY**
1. Hat-making. They are called the Hatters.
2. Uruguayan born Danny Bergara (1991/92 Autoglass Trophy Final).
3. Having adopted World Cup winning Argentina's colours in 1978, they dropped them when the UK went to war with Argentina over the Falkland Islands.
**BRIAN LABONE**
1. Getting married.
2. "One Evertonian is worth twenty Liverpudlians".
3. Jack Charlton.

### "YOU'LL NEVER TAKE THE HOME END!" – II
1. Villa Park, Aston Villa.
2. London Rd, Peterborough.
3. Kenilworth Rd, Luton.

### SOME ANSWERS ABOUT... NEWPORT COUNTY
1. Newcastle.
2. John Aldridge.
3. Ronnie Radford.

### THE 1990s – IV
1. Wolves.
2. Martin O'Neill.
3. The 'Double' (Premier League and FA Cup).

### STRIKING FOR GLORY – IV
1. MacDougall (Norwich), Hales (Charlton), McNeil (Hereford) and Moore (Tranmere).
2. Ronaldo (Brazil 15 goals) and Gerd Müller (W. Germany 14 goals).
3. Brian Deane.

### SOME ANSWERS ABOUT... BOLTON WANDERERS
1. 69 seasons. A record for a club who have never won the championship.
2. Phil Neal.
3. To date, there has never been one.

### FA CUP – IV
1. Numbered shirts.
2. Blackburn.
3. Player/manager Denis Wise (aged 37 years and 158 days).

### STARTING XI – III
Leeds (2000/01).

### SOME ANSWERS ABOUT... BAYERN MUNICH
1. Gerd Muller.
2. Owen Hargreaves.
3. Bixente Lizarazu.

### A WORLD BEATING FOREIGN LEGION
Barthez (Man U), Desailly, Leboeuf and Deschamps (Chelsea), Petit (Arsenal & Chelsea), Karembeu (Middlesbrough) Djorkaeff (Bolton & Blackburn) Guivarc'h (Newcastle), Vieira (Arsenal), Dugarry (Birmingham).

### GETTING THERE – IV
St Mary's Stadium, Southampton.

### SOME ANSWERS ABOUT... LINCOLN CITY
1. Graham Taylor.
2. All five seasons. They lost two finals and three semi-finals.
3. Tony Woodcock.

### THE 1980s – IV
1. Norwich and Sunderland.
2. Walsall and first-timers Birmingham.
3. George Graham.

**HOW MUCH? – IV**

1. Shrewsbury.
2. Juventus.
3. David Mills.

**SOME ANSWERS ABOUT... COVENTRY CITY**

1. Bicycles.
2. He changed their kit from all-white with blue trim to all-sky blue.
3. 34.

**HOME OF THE BRAVE – IV**

1. Ferranti Thistle (1943-1974) and Meadowbank Thistle (1974-1995).
2. None.
3. Never.

**SEQUENCES – IV**

1. Forfar (Bottom of Scottish Division 3 between 2005 and 2008).
2. Jock Stein (Leeds managers from 1961 and 1978).
3. Uruguay (First four winners of the World Cup between 1930 and 1950).

**SOME ANSWERS ABOUT... SCUNTHORPE UNITED**

1. 1988.
2. Jack Cork – son of Alan.
3. Kevin Keegan, Ray Clemence and Ian Botham (at cricket).

**EUROPEAN SILVERWARE – IV**

1. Juventus.
2. Carlos Tevez (Man Utd) and Michael Ballack (Chelsea).
3. Celtic (1970), Leeds (1975), Liverpool (1985 and 2007), Arsenal (2006) and Chelsea (2008).

**THE BIG JOB – II**

1. Ron Greenwood (1961-74) Lyall (74-89) Lou Macari (1989/90).
2. Roy McFarland (1984) Cox (84-93) Roy McFarland (1993-95).
3. Graham Taylor (1987-90) Venglos (90-91) Ron Atkinson (1991-94).

**SOME ANSWERS ABOUT... TURKEY**

1. Brazil.
2. Muzzy Izzet and Colin Kazim-Richards.
3. Rustu Recbar.

**THE 1970s – IV**

1. Billy Bremner.
2. Shrewsbury.
3. Southport, Hereford, Cambridge, Aldershot and Newport.

**BY MUTUAL CONSENT? – IV**

Tommy Docherty. Played for Celtic, Preston, Arsenal and Chelsea. Managed Chelsea, Rotherham, QPR (twice), Aston Villa, Porto, Scotland, Man Utd, Derby, Sydney Olympic (twice), Preston, South Melbourne, Wolves and Altrincham.

**SOME ANSWERS ABOUT... SHREWSBURY TOWN**
1. Scunthorpe, Colchester and Gillingham.
2. Harry Shearer. Voice artiste for 'The Simpsons'. He also played bassist Derek Smalls in 'This Is Spinal Tap', and for many scenes wore a Shrewsbury Town retro shirt.
3. William 'Dixie' Dean.
**THE WORLD GAME – IV**
1. César Luis Menotti (Managed Argentina to World Cup victory in 1978).
2. Marcello Lippi (Never capped as a full international but the only one to win a major prize – the World Cup in 2006).
3. El Salvador and Honduras.

Page 72

**... WAIT A MINUTE MR POSTMAN! – I**
1. Liberty Stadium, Swansea.
2. KC Stadium, Hull.
3. City of Manchester Stadium, Man C.
**SOME ANSWERS ABOUT... SHEFFIELD WEDNESDAY**
1. Because Hillsborough is situated in the Sheffield suburb of Owlerton.
2. Jack Charlton (Republic of Ireland), Howard Wilkinson (England caretaker) and Terry Yorath (Wales and Lebanon).
3. Because they had been drawn away in every round of the cup and had worn these 'lucky' away colours. They lost the final 3-2.
**PETER SCHMEICHEL**
1. Poland.
2. Five.
3. Brad Friedel (Blackburn) and Paul Robinson (Spurs).

Page 73

**SIGN ON THE DOTTED LINE, SON – IV**
1. Brentford.
2. Charlton.
3. Arsenal.
**SOME ANSWERS ABOUT... BRAZIL**
1. Hungary.
2. Gerson.
3. Garrincha and Pelé.
**THE 1960s – IV**
1. Leyton Orient.
2. Peterborough.
3. Northampton.

Page 74

**WHAT'S THAT ON THE FRONT OF YOUR SHIRT? – I**
1. Barnet.
2. Leeds.
3. West Ham.
**SOME ANSWERS ABOUT... SWANSEA CITY**
1. Wigan.
2. Frank Lampard.
3. Both scored hat-tricks on their debuts for the Swans.

**THREE LIONS – IV**
1. Charlie George. Clough and Lampard both gained 2 caps.
2. 41 years and 8 months.
3. FIFA.

**STAT-TASTIC – IV**
Denis Law: Huddersfield, Man C, Torino, Man Utd and Man C again.
**SOME ANSWERS ABOUT... BOURNEMOUTH**
1. Bournemouth and Boscombe Athletic.
2. 2 mins 20 secs.
3. George Best.
**CARLOS TEVEZ**
1. a) "The Argentine prophet for the 21st century."
2. Man Utd.
3. Corinthians.

**OLD GROUNDS FOR NEW – II**
1. Wycombe.
2. Yeovil.
3. Wimbledon.
**SOME ANSWERS ABOUT... BARCELONA**
1. Real Madrid and Athletic Bilbao.
2. Leo Beenhakker.
3. a) He could never play for a club associated with General Franco.
**PRE-1960s – IV**
1. Jack Charlton (Leeds v Doncaster).
2. Everton. They won the title in 1914/15 and also in 1938/39.
3. Portsmouth (1949/50) Spurs (1950/51) Arsenal (1952/53) and Chelsea (1954/55).

**EURO '96 AND ALL THAT – II**
1. Alan Shearer (England v Switzerland).
2. Stefan Kuntz.
3. Bulgaria, Croatia, Czech Republic, Russia, Switzerland and Turkey.
**SOME ANSWERS ABOUT... BARNET**
1. Jimmy Greaves.
2. Stan Flashman. He frequently sacked Fry and then re-instate him.
3. 5-5.
**EURO CHAMPIONSHIPS – IV**
1. By the toss of a coin. The USSR captain Albert Shesternyov called incorrectly.
2. CIS (Commonwealth of Independent States).
3. Spain.

**ODD ONE OUT – II**
Everton.

**SOME ANSWERS ABOUT... WATFORD**
1. Dave Bassett.
2. Luther Blissett. (503 apps – 186 goals).
3. David James.
**TODAY'S THE DAY – IV**
April 12th 1961. In Vostok 1, Yuri Gagarin becomes the first man in space.

**ME! ME! ME! – V**
Jürgen Klinsmann: Played for Stuttgarter Kickers, VfBStuttgart, Inter Milan, Monaco, Spurs (twice), Bayern Munich, Sampdoria and Orange County Blue Star. Managed Germany and Bayern Munich.
**SOME ANSWERS ABOUT... CHESTER CITY**
1. Promotion. (Finally achieved in their 38th season of league football).
2. Moss Rose, Macclesfield.
3. Terry Owen, father of Michael.
**THE 2000s – V**
1. The Walkers Bowl.
2. Layer Road.
3. Hereford (Graham Turner).

**THEME CHOONS**
1. Leicester. Colchester and Peterborough have also used it in the past.
2. Everton and Watford.
3. Crystal Palace.
**SOME ANSWERS ABOUT... HUDDERSFIELD TOWN**
1. 7-6 to Charlton.
2. Denis Law.
3. Arsenal.
**WORLD CUP – V**
1. Black.
2. He scored Israel's only goal, to date, in the World Cup finals.
3. Coffee. They lost 4-2.

**HE SAID WHAT? – IV**
1. Ashley Cole.
2. Pelé.
3. Jose Mourinho (on Frank Lampard).
**SOME ANSWERS ABOUT... GRIMSBY TOWN**
1. Lawrie McMenemy.
2. Graham Taylor.
3. Dr Henry Kissinger.
**STEVE BRUCE**
1. Peter Beardsley.
2. Scored an own-goal.
3. Sheff Utd, Huddersfield, Crystal Palace, Birmingham and Wigan (twice).

**WHO'S MISSING? -III**
Terry Phelan, Alan Cork and Dennis Wise.
**SOME ANSWERS ABOUT... ARSENAL**
1. Holloway.
2. Arsenal in 1999/2000. (Lost to Galatasaray in the UEFA Cup Final).
3. Dave Sexton.
**THE 1990s – V**
1. Assistant Manager to Howard Kendall at the same club.
2. George Burley as manager.
3. Victory in the FA Cup Final where they beat Liverpool 1-0.

**STRIKING FOR GLORY – V**
1. Jairzinho.
2. 142.
3. 7-4 to Portsmouth and 6-4 to Spurs.
**SOME ANSWERS ABOUT... HAMILTON ACADEMICAL**
1. The first players in the UK from behind the 'Iron Curtain'.
2. Alan Rough 1988/89 (5 apps) and Andy Goram 2001/02 (1 app).
3. David Moyes.
**FA CUP – V**
1. Darlington. They were knocked out in the 2nd Round by Gillingham, but when Man Utd opted to play in the Club World Championship, they were reinstated as 'lucky losers'. They lost to Aston Villa in 3rd Round.
2. Highfield Road.
3. 26 – 0.

**WHAT'S IN A NICKNAME? – II**
Darlington. 'The Quakers'.
**SOME ANSWERS ABOUT... BARROW**
1. Wolves.
2. Brian Kidd (Man Utd) They won the European Cup on his 19th birthday.
3. They were voted out.
**SURNAMES**
1. Cole.
2. Jones.
3. Ferdinand.

**GETTING THERE – V**
Blundell Park, Grimsby.
**SOME ANSWERS ABOUT... SWINDON TOWN**
1. 9-1.
2. The FA had stated that only winners from Division 1 could take part.
3. Ossie Ardiles.
**THE 1980s – V**
1. Newport.
2. Bristol R (champions) and Bristol C (runner-up).
3. Plymouth.

**THAT'S MY BOY! – I**
1. Alex (East Stirling) and Darren (Peterborough).
2. Brian (Hartlepool) and Nigel (Burton).
3. Alan Snr (Halifax) and Alan Jnr (Blackpool).
**SOME ANSWERS ABOUT... NOTTINGHAM FOREST**
1. Arsenal.
2. Brian Clough and Frank Clark.
3. Malmo (1978/79) and Hamburg (1979/80).
**HOME OF THE BRAVE – V**
1. Dundee Utd.
2. Celtic Park, Ibrox, Pittodrie, Rugby Park and Tynecastle.
3. Aberdeen (3 times) Hearts (twice), Dundee Utd, Dundee and Kilmarnock (once each).

**SEQUENCES – V**
1. Marcello Lippi (World Cup winning coaches between 1994 and 2006).
2. stadium:mk (The last four homes of Wimbledon/MK Dons).
3. Sven-Göran Eriksson (Man C managers between 1998 and 2008).
**SOME ANSWERS ABOUT... GERMANY**
1. Euro '76 Final against Czechoslovakia.
2. Both were suspended having picked-up yellow cards in the semi-finals.
3. .W. Germany (1950-1990), E. Germany (1950-1990) and Saarland (1950-1956).
**EUROPEAN SILVERWARE – V**
1. A London XI.
2. The Dutch Cup Final had been between Ajax and PSV Eindhoven who both qualified for the newly expanded Champions League. SC Heerenveen won a playoff.
3. Wes Brown, Rio Ferdinand, Owen Hargreaves, Paul Scholes, Michael Carrick, Wayne Rooney, John Terry, Ashley Cole, Frank Lampard and Joe Cole.

**ANOTHER BITE AT THE CHERRY? – III**
Paul Reaney, Billy Bremner, Jack Charlton, Norman Hunter and Johnny Giles.
**SOME ANSWERS ABOUT... MAIDSTONE UNITED**
1. Dartford.
2. Gavin Peacock's father Keith.
3. Aldershot.
**THE 1970s – V**
1. Norwich.
2. Graham Kelly.
3. Gordon Banks.

**BY MUTUAL CONSENT? – V**
Gianluca Vialli. Played for Cremonese, Sampdoria, Juventus. Player/manager at Chelsea. Manager at Watford. QPR allegedly approached him to take over.

**SOME ANSWERS ABOUT... BURNLEY**
1. Aston Villa.
2. Jimmy Adamson.
3. Accrington Stanley.
**SLAVEN BILIC**
1. Harry Redknapp.
2. Everton.
3. Croatia U-21 (together with Aljoša Asanovic).

**HOW MUCH? – V**
1. Alan Ball (Everton to Arsenal). It beat Martin Peters' transfer the previous year by £20,000.
2. Ade Akinbiyi.
3. Parma.
**SOME ANSWERS ABOUT... DONCASTER ROVERS**
1. Burning down Belle Vue's main stand and collecting the insurance money.
2. Man Utd.
3. 'The Comedians'.
**THE WORLD GAME – V**
1. '14' – in honour of Johan Cruyff.
2. 'The Yellow Submarine'.
3. Otto Rehhagel (Greece manager at Euro 2004).

**SIGN ON THE DOTTED LINE, SON – V**
1. Norwich.
2. Watford.
3. Bournemouth.
**SOME ANSWERS ABOUT... ARGENTINA**
1. Sergio Goycochea.
2. Hernán Crespo.
3. Colombia and Spain.
**THE 1960s – V**
1. Man C (champions) and Man Utd (runners-up).
2. Tommy Smith.
3. QPR (Division 1) and Fulham (Division 2).

**STARTING XI – IV**
Derby (1969/70).
**SOME ANSWERS ABOUT... LEEDS UNITED**
1. Jack Charlton.
2. Allan Clarke, Eddie Gray and Billy Bremner.
3. 45 days.
**THREE LIONS – V**
1. 90 times.
2. Highbury. England won 6-1.
3. Walter Winterbottom and Ron Greenwood.

**STAT-TASTIC – V**
Laurie Cunningham: Leyton Orient, WBA, Real Madrid, Man Utd, Sporting de Gijón, Olympique Marseille, Leicester, Rayo Vallecano (twice), Charleroi and Wimbledon.
**SOME ANSWERS ABOUT... MILTON KEYNES DONS**
1. Barnet, Luton and QPR.
2. The National Hockey Stadium.
3. Trophies, including the replica FA Cup, and all memorabilia connected to Wimbledon FC.
**LIAM BRADY**
1. West Ham.
2. Michel Platini.
3. He loved chips.

**... WAIT A MINUTE MR POSTMAN! – II**
1. Keepmost Stadium, Doncaster.
2. Memorial Stadium, Bristol R.
3. Adams Park, Wycombe.
**SOME ANSWERS ABOUT... LUTON TOWN**
1. David Pleat.
2. Raddy Antic.
3. 10. It remains a Football League record for a single match.
**PRE-1960s – V**
1. Kaiserslautern.
2. William 'Dixie' Dean.
3. Billy Wright (Wolves).

**1966 AND ALL THAT... – III**
1. Villa Park, Goodison Park, Wembley, White City, Old Trafford, Ayresome Park, Hillsborough and Roker Park.
2. Uruguay (1930) and Italy (1934).
3. Because there was greyhound racing booked for the same night and Wembley Stadium refused to cancel it.
**SOME ANSWERS ABOUT... TORQUAY UNITED**
1. Forsyth would later marry the former Mrs Stubbs, Anthea Redfearn.
2. West Ham.
3. The Premier League was formed and consequently the divisions below effectively 'moved up' one.
**EURO CHAMPIONSHIPS – V**
1. Sporting Lisbon.
2. USSR (Won one – lost three).
3. Heysel Stadium, Brussels.

**"YOU'LL NEVER TAKE THE HOME END!" – III**
1. Maine Rd, Man C.
2. Stamford Bridge, Chelsea.
3. Loftus Rd, QPR.

**SOME ANSWERS ABOUT... LEYTON ORIENT**
1. Laurie Cunningham.
2. Orient.
3. Wembley Stadium. They played Brentford (att. 10,000) and Southend (att. 2,500).
**TODAY'S THE DAY – V**
December 8th 1980. Mark David Chapman shoots and kills John Lennon.

**ME! ME! ME! – VI**
Thierry Henry has played for Monaco, Juventus, Arsenal and Barcelona.
**SOME ANSWERS ABOUT... JUVENTUS**
1. 'The Big Derby' between Juventus and Torino.
2. Nottingham. His friend supported Notts Co.
3. Cesare Maldini.
**THE 2000s – VI**
1. Dagenham & Redbridge and Morecambe.
2. James Vaughan (Everton) aged 16 years and 271 days, against Crystal Palace.
3. Leicester and Wolves.

**BENCHWARMING – II**
1. Arsenal v Liverpool (1971).
2. Man Utd v Liverpool (1977).
3. Ipswich v Arsenal (1978).
**SOME ANSWERS ABOUT... CHESTERFIELD**
1. Bob Wilson (Arsenal).
2. Middlesbrough.
3. Sheff Wed, Notts Co and Nott'm Forest.
**WORLD CUP – VI**
1. 42.
2. 13.
3. Croatia.

**HE SAID WHAT? – V**
1. Kenny Dalglish resigns from Liverpool in 1991.
2. David Icke.
3. Alan Partridge (Steve Coogan) – commentating on a thunderbolt goal.
**SOME ANSWERS ABOUT... IPSWICH TOWN**
1. One. It was their first season at that level.
2. West Ham.
3. Alf Ramsey, Bobby Robson and George Burley.
**JOHN TERRY**
1. Nott'm Forest.
2. Marcel Desailly.
3. It was the first senior England goal scored at the new Wembley Stadium.

**CUP FINAL COLOURS – II**

1. Red and black striped shirts, black shorts and socks.

2. Gold shirts, white shorts and blue and gold hooped socks.

3. Maroon with white pinstripe shirts, white shorts and maroon socks.

**SOME ANSWERS ABOUT... HEART OF MIDLOTHIAN**

1. Celtic.

2. Murrayfield Stadium,

3. Derby.

**THE 1990s – VI**

1. Spurs won League Cup, and Newcastle were FA Cup runners-up to double-winning Man Utd.

2. No one because bankrupt Aldershot had resigned from the Football League before the season had finished.

3. Carling.

**STRIKING FOR GLORY – VI**

1. Ian Rush (5 goals).

2. At 42 he broke his own record, set four years earlier, as the oldest scorer at a World Cup tournament.

3. Greaves (Chelsea), Clough (Middlesbrough), Towers (Brentford) and Rowley (Shrewsbury).

**SOME ANSWERS ABOUT... BOSTON UNITED**

1. Jim Smith.

2. Paul Gascoigne.

3. Wigan.

**FA CUP – VI**

1. They won the cup with all-English born teams.

2. Newcastle (Stokoe) and Man C (Revie).

3. Both matches were money-spinning derbies. (Arsenal v Spurs and Sheff Wed v Sheff Utd).

**PRAWN SANDWICH ANYONE? – III**

1. Leicester (Humperdinck) v Wolves (Holder).

2. Spurs (Rushdie) v Aston Villa (Osbourne).

3. West Ham (Winstone) v Oxford (Henman).

**SOME ANSWERS ABOUT... ASTON VILLA**

1. 14.

2. Hearts and Rangers.

3. David O'Leary. He was born in Stoke Newington, London.

**MURPHY'S DRAGONS**

1. Temporary manager of Man Utd. Matt Busby was still recovering from the Munich air crash.

2. John & Mel Charles and Ivor & Len Allchurch.

3. Pelé.

**GETTING THERE – VI**
Stadium:mk, MK Dons.
**SOME ANSWERS ABOUT... GREECE**
1. 22. They lost all three group games without scoring.
2. Stelios Giannakopoulos (Bolton).
3. Billy Bingham.
**THE 1980s – VI**
1. Bob Stokoe. He couldn't save them.
2. Alan Shearer.
3. Dario Gradi.

**AT THE MOVIES – II**
1. The Football Factory (2004).
2. The Miracle of Bern (2003).
3. Bend It Like Beckham (2002).
**SOME ANSWERS ABOUT... BRADFORD CITY**
1. The third FA Cup trophy. It was made in Bradford, and City coincidentally became its first winners.
2. Ray Wilson.
3. Odsal Stadium.
**HOME OF THE BRAVE – VI**
1. Stenhousemuir v Ross Co.
2. Raith, based in Kirkcaldy, not only won the Scottish League Division 1 title, they also beat Celtic in the Scottish League Cup Final.
3. Dundee (1987/88), Celtic (1990/91) and Motherwell (1994/95).

**SEQUENCES – VI**
1. Andy Roxburgh (Scotland managers between 1977 and 1993).
2. Gary Lineker (Presenters of 'Match of the Day' from the late '60s to the present day).
3. Exeter (Promoted to the Football League via the play-offs between 2005 and 2008).
**SOME ANSWERS ABOUT... CRYSTAL PALACE**
1. Terry Venables and Peter Taylor (caretaker manager of England).
2. Gary O'Reilly.
3. To represent England as a full international whilst playing for a club outside the top two divisions.
**EUROPEAN SILVERWARE – VI**
1. 758.
2. 45,000.
3. Juventus, Ajax and Bayern Munich.

**ANOTHER BITE AT THE CHERRY? – IV**
Billy McNeill, Tommy Gemmell, Bobby Murdoch, Bertie Auld, Jimmy Johnstone, Bobby Lennox and Willie Wallace.

**SOME ANSWERS ABOUT... USA**
1. Colchester.
2. Haiti.
3. Coventry.
**THE 1970s – VI**
1. Wilf McGuinness. He had taken over from Sir Matt Busby.
2. Huddersfield.
3. Ray Clemence and Kevin Keegan.

Page 107

**BY MUTUAL CONSENT? – VI**
Jim Smith. Played for Sheff Utd, Aldershot, Halifax and Lincoln. Player/manager at Boston and Colchester. Managed Blackburn, Birmingham, Oxford (twice), QPR, Newcastle, Portsmouth and Derby. Assistant at Coventry, Portsmouth and Southampton.
**SOME ANSWERS ABOUT... HARTLEPOOL UNITED**
1. Keith Houchen.
2. Brian Clough.
3. Middlesbrough.
**THE WORLD GAME – VI**
1. Crystal Palace.
2. Democratic Republic of Congo.
3. The first international match played between two non-British European countries.

Page 108

**HOW MUCH? – VI**
1. Chris Sutton (Norwich to Blackburn – £5m) Alan Shearer was his strike-partner.
2. Robbie Keane.
3. Kevin Keegan (Liverpool to Hamburg).
**SOME ANSWERS ABOUT... WOLVERHAMPTON WANDERERS**
1. Andy Beattie and Tommy Docherty (Scotland), Graham Taylor and Glenn Hoddle (England), Bill McGarry (Saudi) and Mick McCarthy (Republic of Ireland).
2. 1982.
3. The introduction of the European Cup two years later.
**STEVE COPPELL**
1. Tranmere.
2. 28.
3. Man C.

Page 109

**SIGN ON THE DOTTED LINE, SON – VI**
1. Millwall.
2. Chesterfield.
3. Colchester.
**SOME ANSWERS ABOUT... TRANMERE ROVERS**
1. John Aldridge.
2. 13-4.
3. Ron Yeats.

### THE 1960s – VI
1. Diego Maradona.
2. The Division 3 Championship and The League Cup.
3. As players; Venables (Chelsea), Robson (Fulham) and Wilkinson (Sheff Wed). As managers; Greenwood (West Ham) and Mercer (Aston Villa).

Page 110

### THAT'S MY BOY! – II
1. John (Swindon) and Paul (Bristol R).
2. John and Kevin (both Bournemouth).
3. Don (Bristol R) and Gary (Norwich).

### SOME ANSWERS ABOUT... LEICESTER CITY
1. Four finals, four defeats.
2. Martin O'Neill.
3. Martin Allen.

### THREE LIONS – VI
1. 11 years and 2 months.
2. Walter Winterbottom. But the team was selected by a committee.
3. Argentina.

Page 111

### STAT-TASTIC – VI
Ian Wright:: Crystal Palace, Arsenal, West Ham, Nott'm Forest, Celtic and Burnley.

### SOME ANSWERS ABOUT... NOTTS COUNTY
1. No. They were relegated on the last day of the old Division 1.
2. Jermaine Pennant.
3. The River Trent.

### JIMMY JOHNSTONE
1. c) "My nightmare."
2. 'Jinky'.
3. Sheff Utd (1975-1977).

Page 112

### INTO THE LEAGUE! – III
Bolton.

### SOME ANSWERS ABOUT... ITALY
1. W. Germany.
2. Torino. 18 players were killed of which 10 were full internationals for Italy.
3. Man C.

### PRE-1960s – VI
1. Bob Paisley.
2. Genoa.
3. Only Real Madrid. They won it all four times.

Page 113

### EURO '96 AND ALL THAT – III
1. Hristo Stoichkov (Bulgaria), Jürgen Klinsmann (Germany), Davor Šuker (Croatia) and Brian Laudrup (Denmark).
2. Wembley, Old Trafford, Anfield, Villa Park, Elland Road, Hillsborough, St James' Park and The City Ground.
3. Ally McCoist.

**SOME ANSWERS ABOUT... COLCHESTER UNITED**
1. Fog.
2. It was a wind-assisted punt downfield by goalkeeper Scott Barrett.
3. Steve Cram. His uncle was Bobby Cram.
**EURO CHAMPIONSHIPS – VI**
1. Norway.
2. Alan Mullery, Cyril Knowles and Jimmy Greaves. Only Mullery played.
3. Stadio Olimpico (Rome).

Page 114

**OLD GROUNDS FOR NEW – III**
1. Chester.
2. Newport.
3. Bolton.
**SOME ANSWERS ABOUT... INTER MILAN**
1. Real Madrid (5 times), Benfica (twice) and AC Milan (once).
2. Roy Hodgson.
3. None. They are the only club to be constant members.
**TODAY'S THE DAY – VI**
February 11th 1975. Margaret Thatcher defeats Edward Heath and becomes leader of the Conservative Party.

Page 115

**ME! ME! ME! – VII**
David Beckham: Man U, Preston (loan), Real Madrid and LA Galaxy.
**SOME ANSWERS ABOUT... FULHAM**
1. Johnny Haynes.
2. Ray Wilkins (Manager) and Kevin Keegan (Chief Operating Officer).
3. All three were caretaker-managers who didn't take the job full-time.
**THE 2000s – VII**
1. 'Deadly' Doug Ellis.
2. Southend (champions) and Colchester (runners-up) won promotion to the Championship (2nd tier).
3. For the first time in Premier League history, all three of the promoted clubs survived.

Page 116

**CLIMBING UP THE PYRAMID**
1. Colchester and Doncaster.
2. Colne Dynamoes.
3. Altrincham.
**SOME ANSWERS ABOUT... SOUTHPORT**
1. Stan Mortensen (3 goals) and Bill Perry (the winning goal).
2. Billy Bingham.
3. The Vulcan Motor Company. Southport became the first club to take a sponsors name.
**WORLD CUP – VII**
1. Lehmann (Germany), A.Cole, Campbell, Walcott (England), Ljungberg (Sweden), Touré, Eboué (Ivory Coast), van Persie (Holland), Gilberto Silva (Brazil), Henry (France), Djourou, Senderos (Switzerland), Adebayor (Togo) Reyes, Fàbregas (Spain).
2. 199,954.
3. It is believed to have been melted down.

**SKIPPER! – II**
1. Leicester v Tranmere (1999/2000 League Cup Final).
2. Greece v Portugal (Euro 2004 Final).
3. Bayern Munich v Bordeaux (1995/96 UEFA Cup Final).
**SOME ANSWERS ABOUT... LIVERPOOL**
1. Juventus, Bayern Munich and Benfica.
2. One. The UEFA Cup in 1972/73.
3. The Boot Room. It stored the players boots.
**GERD MÜLLER**
1. 68.
2. Franz Beckenbauer and Sepp Maier.
3. 'Der Bomber'.

**WHO'S MISSING? – IV**
David Platt, Tony Adams and Steve McManaman.
**SOME ANSWERS ABOUT... BRENTFORD**
1. Rod Stewart.
2. None. They won all 21 games.
3. QPR. The fans and a £104,000 loan from a future chairman successfully saw-off this merger.
**THE 1990s – VII**
1. Tomas Brolin.
2. Sir John Hall.
3. Tony Barton.

**STRIKING FOR GLORY – VII**
1. Colombia were knocked out of the tournament and Escobar was murdered on his return home.
2. 13. It is a record that still stands.
3. Yugoslavia (1990) and Croatia (1998).
**SOME ANSWERS ABOUT... WALSALL**
1. Allan Clarke.
2. Arsenal, managed by Herbert Chapman.
3. Trinidad and Tobago.
**FA CUP – VII**
1. Gary Lineker.(Spurs).
2. 'The Invincibles'.
3. Stan Seymour (Newcastle), Terry Venables (Spurs), Kenny Dalglish (Liverpool) and George Graham (Arsenal).

**LATIN HOMEWORK – II**
1. Sunderland – Pursuit of Excellence.
2. Bury – Effort Overcomes All.
3. Tranmere – Where there is Faith, there is Light and Strength.

### SOME ANSWERS ABOUT... PORT VALE
1. Stanley Matthews.
2. Division 3 (South).
3. 'The Wembley of the North'.
### THREE LIONS ALTERNATIVE STRIP
1. All light blue.
2. Yellow shirts, navy blue shorts, yellow socks.
3. All grey. (Though, according to the FA, it was officially indigo blue).

Page 121

### GETTING THERE – VII
Tynecastle, Hearts.
### SOME ANSWERS ABOUT... SHEFFIELD UNITED
1. Joe Mercer.
2. An audience with Pope John Paul II.
3. Sheff Utd was founded in 1889 at the Adelphi Hotel, which was demolished to make way for the Crucible Theatre. The World Snooker Championship has been held there since 1977.
### THE 1980s – VII
1. Crystal Palace and Wimbledon.
2. Norman Whiteside.
3. Mark Lawrenson.

Page 122

### ... WAIT A MINUTE MR POSTMAN – III
1. Bloomfield Rd, Blackpool.
2. Field Mill, Mansfield.
3. Boundary Park, Oldham.
### SOME ANSWERS ABOUT... QUEEN OF THE SOUTH
1. Dumfries.
2. Robert Duvall (the coach) and Michael Keaton (the owner).
3. Hughie Gallacher.
### HOME OF THE BRAVE – VII
1. Inverness Caladonian Thistle.
2. Gretna.
3. Goalkeeper.

Page 123

### SEQUENCES – VII
1. Sven-Göran Eriksson (The last four managers to take England to the World Cup finals).
2. Hull (Promoted through the play-offs to the Premier League between 2005 and 2008).
3. Stadium of Light (As of 2008, they are the four largest club stadiums in England).
### SOME ANSWERS ABOUT... DERBY COUNTY
1. Disgraced chairman and media mogul, Robert Maxwell.
2. Tommy Docherty and George Burley.
3. The Brian Clough Trophy.

**EUROPEAN SILVERWARE – VII**
1. Wolves (1972), Dundee Utd (1987), Arsenal (2000), Celtic (2003), Middlesbrough (2006) and Rangers (2008).
2. Ronaldo (Sporting Lisbon), Tevez (Boca Juniors), Rooney (Everton) and Vidic (Red Star Belgrade).
3. Sven-Göran Eriksson.

Page 124

**BENCHWARMING – III**
1. Man Utd v Liverpool (1982/83).
2. Man C v WBA (1969/70).
3. Leeds v Arsenal (1967/68).
**SOME ANSWERS ABOUT... GATESHEAD**
1. South Shields.
2. St James' Park, Newcastle.
3. Peterborough.
**THE 1970s – VII**
1. Eric Sykes.
2. Bremner (Doncaster), Charlton (Sheff Wed), Clarke (Barnsley), Giles (Republic of Ireland and Shamrock) and Revie (United Arab Emirates).
3. Crewe.

Page 125

**BY MUTUAL CONSENT? – VII**
Bill Shankly. Played for Carlisle and Preston. Managed Carlisle, Grimsby, Workington, Huddersfield and Liverpool.
**SOME ANSWERS ABOUT... HOLLAND**
1. Rinus Michels and Johan Cruyff.
2. W. Germany and Argentina.
3. Edwin van der Sar.
**THE WORLD GAME – VII**
1. Santos.
2. 'The Meat'.
3. Olympique Lyonnais (Lyon).

Page 126

**WHAT'S IN A NICKNAME? – III**
Plymouth or Boston. 'The Pilgrims'.
**SOME ANSWERS ABOUT...CREWE ALEXANDRA**
1. a) Princess Alexandra.
2. Neil Lennon. He had made one appearance for Man C.
3. Spurs.
**LUIS FIGO**
1. Johan Cruyff.
2. A pig's head.
3. Sporting Lisbon.

Page 127

**SIGN ON THE DOTTED LINE, SON – VII**
1. Arsenal.
2. Derby.
3. Blackpool.

**SOME ANSWERS ABOUT... WREXHAM**
1. Anderlecht.
2. Ian Rush.
3. Scotland. Wales lost 2-0.
**THE 1960s – VII**
1. George Best. It translates as 'The Fifth Beatle'.
2. Don Revie (Leeds), Brian Clough (Derby Co), Ken Furphy (Watford) Lawrie McMenemy (Doncaster). All four were born in the North-East of England.
3. Arthur Turner.

Page 128

**TAKING THE MIC – II**
Brian Moore.
**SOME ANSWERS ABOUT... MELCHESTER ROVERS**
1. 1954.
2. Because their stadium, Mel Park, had been struck by an earthquake.
3. Red and yellow.
**THREE LIONS – VII**
1. Kevin Keegan and Steve McClaren.
2. 22 years and 8 months.
3. Jamie Redknapp.

Page 129

**STAT-TASTIC – VII**
Trevor Francis: Birmingham, Detroit Express, Nott'm Forest, Man C, Sampdoria, Atalanta, Rangers, QPR and Sheff Wed.
**SOME ANSWERS ABOUT... MANSFIELD TOWN**
1. Bobby Moore, Martin Peters, Geoff Hurst and Trevor Brooking.
2. One. They were relegated at the end of their only season.
3. Luther Blissett.
**JEFF ASTLE**
1. Brazil.
2. The manager was Barry Fry and the player was George Best.
3. The first player to score in both major domestic cup finals held at Wembley – the FA Cup and the League Cup.

Page 130

**HOW MUCH? – VII**
1. Winstone Bogarde.
2. Steve Daley and Andy Gray.
3. Jean-Pierre Papin.
**SOME ANSWERS ABOUT... PRESTON NORTH END**
1. Bobby Charlton, Nobby Stiles and Brian Kidd (Man Utd).
2. Tom Finney (England – 76 caps).
3. Wolves.
**PRE-1960s – VII**
1. Arbroath 36 Bon Accord 0. A British record.
2. Terry Paine (Southampton).
3. Belenenses.

**1966 AND ALL THAT – IV**
1. Africa. Only one place had been allocated for both Africa and Asia.
2. Jimmy Greaves (Spurs), John Connelly (Man Utd), Ron Springett (Sheff Wed), Peter Bonetti (Chelsea), Jimmy Armfield (Blackpool), Gerry Byrne (Liverpool), Ron Flowers (Wolves), Norman Hunter (Leeds), Terry Paine (Southampton), Ian Callaghan (Liverpool), George Eastham (Arsenal).
3. N. Korea 3 Portugal 0 – Portugal eventually won 5-3.
**SOME ANSWERS ABOUT... YEOVIL TOWN**
1. Alec Stock.
2. Latvia.
3. Ian Botham.
**EURO CHAMPIONSHIPS – VII**
1. Gerd Müller.
2. David James, Paul Robinson and Ian Walker.
3. None at all.

**NET MINDERS – ii**
Marriott (Sunderland), Gerrard (Everton), Hislop (West Ham), Harper (Newcastle), James (Aston Villa), Poom (Derby), Walker (Spurs), Seaman (Arsenal), Flowers (Leicester), Srnicek (Sheff Wed), Westerveld (Liverpool), Chamberlain (Watford), Clarke (Bradford C), Martyn (Leeds), Jones (Southampton) and Sullivan (Wimbledon).
**SOME ANSWERS ABOUT... BRIGHTON & HOVE ALBION**
1. Gillingham.
2. Gary Stevens.
3. Steve Gritt and Alan Curbishley (Charlton).
**TODAY'S THE DAY – VII**
February 11th 1990. Nelson Mandela is released.

**ME! ME! ME! – VIII**
Pat Jennings: Newry, Watford, Spurs and Arsenal. He made his international debut alongside George Best.
**SOME ANSWERS ABOUT... PARTICK THISTLE**
1. John Hansen. Brother of Alan.
2. Alan Rough.
3. Mo Johnson.
**THE 2000s – VIII**
1. Chelsea v Man Utd (Charity Shield).
2. Leeds and Huddersfield.
3. First ever visit to Wembley and first ever promotion to the top-flight.

**MR CHAIRMAN – II**
1. Ken Bates (Oldham, Chelsea & Leeds).
2. Tommy Trinder (Fulham).
3. Louis Edwards (Man Utd).

**SOME ANSWERS ABOUT... CHARLTON ATHLETIC**
1. Crystal Palace and West Ham.
2. Diego Maradona.
3. Alan Curbishley's brother Bill.

**WORLD CUP – VIII**
1. Hungary and Brazil.
2. The extra-time golden goal. Hosts France beat Paraguay (Round of 16).
3. In a shoebox under his bed.

Page 135

**HE SAID WHAT? – VI**
1. Diego Maradona.
2. George Best.
3. Norman Whiteside.

**SOME ANSWERS ABOUT... OLDHAM ATHLETIC**
1. Man Utd.
2. Norway.
3. WBA (551 feet) and Port Vale (525 feet).

**CHARLIE NICHOLAS**
1. Liverpool and Man Utd.
2. Perry Groves.
3. 'Champagne Charlie'.

Page 136

**"YOU'LL NEVER TAKE THE HOME END!" – IV**
1. Goodison Park, Everton.
2. Vicarage Rd, Watford.
3. St James's Park, Newcastle.

**SOME ANSWERS ABOUT... DARLINGTON**
1. George Reynolds.
2. Paul Gascoigne and Faustino Asprilla.
3. David Wheater (Middlesbrough).

**THE 1990s – VIII**
1. Steve Gerrard.
2. Neil Warnock.
3. Liverpool, Leeds, Arsenal, Blackburn and Man Utd.

Page 137

**STRIKING FOR GLORY – VIII**
1. Tranmere (1984/85).
2. Bournemouth (1971/72).
3. Newcastle (1982/83).

**SOME ANSWERS ABOUT... HARCHESTER UNITED**
1. Ron Atkinson.
2. He was shot dead by mistake.
3. No.

**FA CUP – VIII**
1. Spurs (Southern League) beat Sheff Utd (Division 1).
2. Chile.
3. QPR (1982), Sunderland (1992), Millwall (2004) and Cardiff (2008).

**STARTING XI – V**
Spurs (1984/85).
**SOME ANSWERS ABOUT... BRISTOL CITY**
1. Three consecutive relegations.
2. Ade Akinbiyi.
3. Andy Cole (£0.5m).
**AT THE MOVIES – III**
1. A Shot at Glory (2000).
2. Mike Bassett: England Manager (2001).
3. The Game of Their Lives (2002).

**GETTING THERE – VIII**
St James' Park, Newcastle.
**SOME ANSWERS ABOUT... CHELSEA**
1. A Chelsea Pensioner.
2. It was the first time in an English league game that a team had taken the field without a single British player in its line-up.
3. Ron Harris (795 apps), Peter Bonetti (729 apps) and John Hollins (592 apps).
**THE 1980s – VIII**
1. Kevin Keegan (Newcastle).
2. Darlington replaced Colchester.
3. Bruce Grobbelaar, Craig Johnston and Mark Lawrenson.

**THE BIG JOB – III**
1. David Webb (1980-82) Megson (83) Harry Redknapp (1983-92).
2. Micky Adams (1996-97) Wilkins (97-98) Kevin Keegan (1998-99).
3. Johnny Giles (1984-85) Saunders (86-87) Ron Atkinson (1987-88).
**SOME ANSWERS ABOUT... PETERBOROUGH UNITED**
1. Simon Davies and Matthew Etherington.
2. Goalkeeper Joe Lewis.
3. 52.
**HOME OF THE BRAVE – VIII**
1. A 3-1 victory by Inverness Caladonian Thistle at Celtic in the 1999/2000 Scottish Cup 3rd Round.
2. 'The Quality Street Kids'.
3. Duncan Ferguson.

**SEQUENCES – VIII**
1. W. Germany (First four winners of the Euro Championships between 1960 and 1972).
2. Gordon Strachan (Last four Celtic managers up to 2008).
3. Geoff Hurst  (Scored the four goals to win the World Cup for England in 1966).
**SOME ANSWERS ABOUT... KIDDERMINSTER HARRIERS**
1. Northampton.
2. Jan Molby.
3. The first club to play at both the old stadium and the new one.

**EUROPEAN SILVERWARE – VIII**
1. Cardiff (1967/68 to 1971/72).
2. Spurs and Wolves. Spurs won 3-2 on aggregate.
3. Giovanni Trapattoni.

Page 142

**HOW MUCH? – VIII**
1. David Platt (Aston Villa to Bari).
2. Graham Souness.
3. Ferenc Puskas. He was denied because of the FA rules regarding employment of foreign players.

**SOME ANSWERS ABOUT... MILLWALL**
1. The first Football League match to be played on a Sunday.
2. Their fan base was largely dockworkers and it allowed them to finish their shift and get to the ground in time for kick-off.
3. Teddy Sheringham.

**THE 1970s – VIII**
1. Dennis Follows.
2. Liverpool ('Hitachi').
3. Steve Coppell.

Page 143

**BY MUTUAL CONSENT? – VIII**
Neil Warnock: Played for Chesterfield, Rotherham, Hartlepool, Scunthorpe, Aldershot, Barnsley, York and Crewe. Managed Gainsborough Trinity, Burton, Scarborough, Notts Co, Torquay, Huddersfield, Plymouth, Oldham, Bury, Sheff Utd and Crystal Palace... so far.

**SOME ANSWERS ABOUT... REAL MADRID**
1. It was the first time it had been won by a team and coach all born in the same country.
2. Only twice (1956/57 & 1957/58).
3. David Beckham.

**THE WORLD GAME – VIII**
1. '10' – the shirt number he would always be associated with.
2. Lothar Matthäus.
3. Indonesia.

Page 144

**LEAGUE CUP – II**
1. Bertie Auld
2. Wembley, Hillsborough (replay) and Old Trafford (2nd replay).
3. Martin O'Neill (Leicester) and John Aldridge (Tranmere).

**SOME ANSWERS ABOUT... DUNDEE UNITED**
1. Walter Smith.
2. They dropped the clubs traditional colours of white and black, and adopted the Tornado's tangerine colours.
3. Barcelona.

**BERT TRAUTMANN**
1. Frank Swift.
2. A broken neck.
3. b) "Hello Fritz. Fancy a cup of tea?"

**SIGN ON THE DOTTED LINE, SON – VIII**
1.Bury.
2. West Ham.
3. Millwall.
**SOME ANSWERS ABOUT... YORK CITY**
1. Division 3 (North).
2. Eamon Dunphy.
3. Phil Boyer and Ted MacDougall.
**THE 1960s – VIII**
1. Northampton.
2. John White.
3. Tony Cascarino and Ruud Gullit.

**OLD GROUNDS FOR NEW – IV**
1. Stoke.
2. Wigan.
3. Oxford.
**SOME ANSWERS ABOUT... ROCHDALE**
1. Stan Milburn. Brother of Jackie and uncle of Bobby and Jack Charlton.
2. Tommy Cannon of Cannon & Ball.
3. 1973/74.
**THREE LIONS – VIII**
1. Automatically. 1966 as hosts and 1970 as champions.
2. Malcolm Macdonald.
3. Don Revie and Bobby Robson.

**STAT-TASTIC – VIII**
David James: Watford, Liverpool, Aston Villa, West Ham, Man C and Portsmouth.
**SOME ANSWERS ABOUT... NORWICH CITY**
1. Robert Earnshaw.
2. Mike Walker.
3. Martin Peters.
**BOBBY MOORE**
1. Malcolm Allison.
2. Spurs.
3. Italy. The scorer was Fabio Capello.

**WHAT'S THAT ON THE FRONT OF YOUR SHIRT? – II**
1. Norwich.
2. Coventry.
3. Chelsea.
**SOME ANSWERS ABOUT... FEYENOORD**
1. Celtic.
2. Clyde Best.
3. His glasses.

**PRE-1960s – VIII**
1. Malcom Allison, Noel Cantwell, John Bond, Dave Sexton and Frank O'Farrell.
2. Roker Park and Highbury.
3. Michel Hidalgo.

Page 149

**1966 AND ALL THAT – V**
1. b) He didn't like the way Rattin had looked at him.
2. Banks (Stoke), Cohen (Fulham), Wilson (Bradford C), Stiles (Preston), J. Charlton (Leeds), Moore (Fulham), Ball (Bristol R), Hunt (Bolton), B. Charlton (Preston), Hurst (WBA) and Peters (Sheff Utd).
3. Portugal and N. Korea.

**SOME ANSWERS ABOUT... PORTUGAL**
1. All four times.
2. Mozambique.
3. Luis Figo.

**EURO CHAMPIONSHIPS – VIII**
1. Greece.
2. Marco van Basten.
3. Johan Neeskens and Johan Cruyff.

Page 150

**INTO THE LEAGUE! – IV**
Scarborough.

**SOME ANSWERS ABOUT...EXETER CITY**
1. Brazil.
2. 0-0.
3. Gerry Francis and Alan Ball.

**TODAY'S THE DAY – VIII**
November 22nd 1963. US President John F. Kennedy is assassinated.

# RECOMMENDED WEBSITE ACKNOWLEDGEMENTS

All Official club websites
historicalkits.co.uk
englandfootballonline.com
footballsite.co.uk
soccerbase.com
fifa.com
givemefootball.com
thefa.com
leaguemanagers.com
archive.timesonline.co.uk
guardian.co.uk
expertfootball.com
Wikipedia